caws & causeries

Caws & Causeries
⇛ around poetry and poets ⇚

Anselm Hollo

For Bov Davis,
remembering
many
good conversations —
in old friendship,
Anselm
1999/2000
≈

LA ALAMEDA PRESS
Albuquerque

Some of these texts, or parts of them, have appeared in *Arshile*,
Black Mountain: American Poetry Lectures ("Sa Nostra" Centre de
Cultura, Palma 1998), *Bombay Gin, Boundary2, Contemporary Authors
Autobiography Series Volume 19, Disembodied Poetics: Annals of the
Jack Kerouac School* (University of New Mexico Press, 1994),
*First Intensity, Gare du Nord, Sulfur, The Electronic Poetry
Center* (Buffalo), *The Kerouac School Newsletter*, and
The Poet's Notebook (W.W. Norton, New York 1995).

The author is grateful to the editors, publishers, printers,
and distributors of these publications. He also wishes to
acknowledge the generous support of the Finnish Cultural
Foundation and the hospitality of the Grez-sur-Loing
Foundation August through December, 1998.

ISBN: 1-888809-15-9
Library of Congress Number: 99-73744

Cover painting: "Crows" (detail) —Yosa Buson
Edo Period, 18th century • *ink & light color on paper*

Frontispiece drawing:
Copyright © 1999 by Jane Dalrymple-Hollo
ink on paper

Author photograph:
Copyright © 1999 by Michael Friedman

La Alameda Press
9636 Guadalupe Trail NW
Albuquerque, New Mexico 87114

Books by Anselm Hollo

POETRY

& It Is a Song
Faces & Forms
The Coherences
Haiku
Tumbleweed
Maya
Sensation 27
Some Worlds
Black Book
Notes & Paramecia
Lingering Tangos
Sojourner Microcosms
Heavy Jars
Lunch in Fur
With Ruth in Mind
Finite Continued
No Complaints
Pick Up the House
Outlying Districts
Space Baltic
Near Miss Haiku
Blue Ceiling
High Beam
West Is Left on the Map
Survival Dancing
Corvus
AHOE (And How on Earth)
AHOE 2 (Johnny Cash Writes
   a Letter to Santa Claus)

SELECTED TRANSLATIONS

Poetry
Some Poems by Paul Klee
Red Cats
William Carlos Williams: Paterson
   (in German, with Josephine Clare)
Allen Ginsberg: Kaddisch und andere
   Gedichte (with J.C.)
Gregory Corso: Gasoline und andere
   Gedichte (with J.C.)
Paavo Haavikko: Selected Poems
Pentti Saarikoski: Selected Poems
The Poems of Hipponax
Pentti Saarikoski: Trilogy

Prose
Jean Genet: Querelle
Franz Innerhofer: Beautiful Days
Olof Lagercrantz: Strindberg
Peter Stephan Jungk: Werfel
Lennart Hagerfors: The Whales in
   Lake Tanganyika
Jaan Kross: The Czar's Madman
Rosa Liksom: One Night Stands
Lars Kleberg: Starfall: A Triptych

Plays & Screenplays
Bertolt Brecht: Jungle of Cities
Georg Büchner: Woyzeck
François Truffaut: Small Change
Louis Malle: Au revoir les enfants

Table of Contents

Author's Note

In the [. . .] Middle Ages, Latinizations of names of non-Latin origin were relatively common. Had I lived then (and especially if I had been born in Hungary instead of Finland), my last name could have been Corvus or Corvinus: in Hungarian, the raven is *hollo*. And Hollo was the name my paternal Finnish great-grandfather adopted after a family dispute whose causes are lost in the murk of time. The word has no lexical meaning in Finnish; it was simply the traditional name of a piece of land he owned. Finnish and Hungarian belong to the Finno-Ugric/Ural-Altaic family of languages and share a relatively small proto-vocabulary; but the modern Finnish for raven is *korppi*, borrowed from Latin *corvus* via Swedish *korpen*. Both raven and corvus derive from the Indo-European root *ker*, "to cry out." (Joseph T. Shipley, The Origins of English Words, Baltimore, 1984) I have always admired that uncompromisingly elegant bird, in all its mythical and legendary manifestations. I even like its *ker*, more appropriate to the poetry of this century than the trills of the nightingale.

(Corvus, 1995)

So—that explains the "caws" part. "Causerie" = informal conversation, short essay: "latter sense first used in *The Edinburgh Review* (19th cent.)." The causerie ("kåseri" in Swedish, "pakina" in Finnish) printed in the daily newspaper was a form I grew up with: less rigidly defined than the U.S.American "column," often humorous but not restricted to trade-mark shtick or routine, the European causerie could be a brief polemic, review, satire, love letter, prose poem. In the first half of the century, two great masters of the form were Austrian: Karl Kraus, a brilliant slayer of cultural shlock dragons, and Peter Altenberg, a classic lover of nightlife and lowlife with his own quite unselfconscious poetics (which remind me of Richard Brautigan):

What is a Poem?
A poem is a device designed to create a mood in the reader that is similar to the mood its author was in composing it. Right—
    Poem: "Early Spring."
    Morning temperature on the Hochschneeberg:
    34 degrees Fahrenheit.
    Precipitation, in the form of rain.
    Damply shimmering whitish-gray snowfields.
    Water rising steadily in the rivers.
    Mild, stormy weather. Generally overcast.
    Continued tremendous snowfall in the
                        Northern Alps.
    Avalanches have blocked Tunnel Nr. 11.
    The hotels of Semmering are overflowing with gentry and wealthy bourgeoise attempting to squeeze in a few more days of tobogganing and such. But the Sun is gobbling up the Snow.
    The Earth is saturated, not to say soggy, which is why the surplus water is rushing into the rivers.
    The farmer is optimistic.
    Young Helga, weeping, is scouring the terrain for primroses.

(Altenberg, 1919)

    Now that I have 'explained' the title of this book and digressed into quoting a long-gone obscure Viennese feuilletonist (=writer of "little leaves": again, causeries), all I have to say about this miscellany of writing with aligned margins is that I hope that it may provide some pleasure, perhaps some salutary irritation, and some insight into what the "graphs of" this "mind moving" (Philip Whalen's description of the poetic act) have been about.

All the individual pieces collected here circle around poetry and poets without necessarily being about or on them. They owe their existence to persons who commissioned or otherwise asked for them; they do not aspire to profound theoretical insight, consistency, correctness, or any other kind of universality. In the arts, there is no "progress" in the techno-scientific sense, and poetry, like the other arts, keeps reinventing the wheel (but once in a while we have to rotate or change the tires (or lyres)!).

My life-in-print has been lived in the world of the small press and little magazines. Existing somewhere between the truly mass-produced and the limited (intentional or unintentional) collector's item, the products of this world are by their very nature eccentric, ephemeral, fugitive. At their best, they carry the kind of 'transmission' that letters exchanged between artists and poets used to convey in past centuries— the kind of transmission that occurs when "occasionally. . . / you do meet someone / . . . on a printed page." (Charles Olson) So—hail, Fellow Stranger, well met. Or, as Ted Berrigan put it in a lecture at The Kerouac School of Poetics:

> I'll tell you what to do while you're waiting for the bus.
> When the bus comes, you're on your own. You're gonna
> have to drive that bus, you might even be that bus, you'll
> also be all the passengers, and then you're gonna run into
> yourself coming the other way. But you'll take care of
> that.

Anselm Hollo
27 May 1999
Boulder

From the Notebooks

ONE OF THE PLEASURES of "notebook" writing is, of course, that the writer is free to make indefensible utterances—and it is then up to her or him, or to authorized literary executors, to censor them (or not). You can say anything. It's all right. The notebook is also a commonplace book, a collection of quotes possibly useful, or curious, or so incredibly stupid that they're worth preserving. These include quotes from oneself. That's the notebook as *sottisier*. Since the advent of the personal computer, I compose much of my writing, including poems, on the screen, but still prefer the notebook to any portable version of my trusty old Mac. From time to time I go through notebook jottings to find the beginnings of a poem or at least a line or two. The poem at the end of this selection, part of a fourteen-sonnet sequence, demonstrates obvious (and some not-so-obvious) gleanings from preceding notebook entries.

1979-1998

"Lampshades! Lampshades!
All sizes! All colors!
Blue for comfort! Red for passion!
Get yourselves a lampshade, Comrades!"
—Mayakovsky, *The Bedbug*

Mina Loy the greater poet designed lampshades
(he writes these essays in his head)

Nobel Prize to be divided in 3 equal parts between:
        h.c. artmann (Austria)
        Paavo Haavikko (Finland)
        Ernesto Cardenal (Nicaragua)

(conveyed to PEN 1-24-80)

If you could find a large enough ocean to hold it,
Saturn would *float*
(radio info)

music: people who really understand it must have a hard time in this
(human, social) world—seeing, feeling, as they must, how terribly *skewed*
that world is—in terms of over-all construction

> "aesthetics
> is for the artist
> as ornithology
> is for the birds"

—Barnett Newman

re: "line breaks":
"She was speaking quietly but fast, and pausing for breath in the wrong
places, the way politicians do when they fear interruption"
                                        —Gavin Lyall, *The Crocus List*

My tribe of poets isn't really "out for scars"
they'd much rather stay in their rooms
giggling over their notebooks

"Satire
is an overloading of meaning
that so burdens the reader's belief
that it collapses,
exploding meaning
and hopefully leading it
in a direction opposite to
its stated intent"
—Daniel Gercke *(Colorado Daily, 2-26-86)*

give me phrase or give me fable

Uninspired
today
my 'inspiration' is like Kit Robinson's cats
First
they moved into the kitchen wall
Then
they were gone

guy looks like a giant molar with arms & legs

Je ne l'ai pas connu
Peter Whigham
but he sure was one hell of a translator
& not a mean poet
like his greatest past voice Catullus
perhaps even too kind
he came my way once
bewildered-bearded
silent & manic like so many of us

Ah, real estate ahoy! it is Columbus Day
the globe is still a globe, the paleface still holds sway
the buck's a buck, a slave's a slave—
etc.

"Anthologies are to poets as the zoo is to animals"
          —David Antin

permanent diaspora—the ideal state
(my sympathies always with the Gypsies
rather than the Zionists or now Palestinians, etc.)

writers of small language groups—their admirable stubbornness in
clinging to the 'absoluteness' of their particular language—*their words*
—by extension, that's of course true of everybody—

"[critics] will always choose poetry which labors to be 'poetic,' whether by remembered forms or by a nostalgic, privately pained tilt of the head and vocal chords. . . "

—Marvin Bell

Ezra Pound's complicated love life
drove him to Economics?

Harper's Index—greatest American 'serial poem' of the Eighties

EP
just a cracker who fell in love with books

All poetry is 'hermetic,' 'cryptic,' heretical use of words—not to sell, not to instruct in skills designed to produce & sell—so, in that sense, *l'art* is always *pour l'art*: the un-paraphrasable is what we want

when "straight talk" was shown to be crooked
& "sincerity" merely as in "yours sincerely"
we got L=A=N=G=U=A=G=E

"Dolphins (as we speak)
are carrying on 2
conversations simultaneously

& within the clicks of one
lie the squeaks of the other

they are alive in their little wandering pool"
                              —Ted Berrigan & Anne Waldman, *Memorial Day*

Le style pompier—the poetry of pompous statement—what *everybody*,
from post-WW 2 Vienna School to the L=A=N=Gs has been trying
to get away from: yet these 'elevated diction' folks (mostly white
Southern, in these States) keep cropping up. . .

"We're all toast, anyway"—dude at Brigham Young University, to
Jane, re: radiation hazards

Translations—often, perhaps always? at least partial mis-hearings—
what happens to every poem when someone else reads it

the "Mac" put Tzara's instructions for Dada poem in "scrapbook"
(can't recall telling it to do so)

"post-national"
(*je suis*)
but also "lower-case american"

"I cut the orange in two, and couldn't make the two parts
equal.
To which was I unjust? I'm going to eat them both!"
                              —Alberto Caeiro (Fernando Pessoa)

attention exactly *between* the words

"No provision for transvestites in Geneva Convention"
"OK—put 'em in a separate tent"
                              —News, Panama, January 1990

The "joys of opacity"—still a post-Romantic yearning for "The
Unnameable"—but Samuel Beckett (now gone) did it better: he's
never "opaque"—& he's still the champ

troubadour tradition: *oppositional* to patriarchal 'mainstream' (even if
'sexist' 'pedestalist' etc.)

getting old when you start noticing how almost impossibly hard the young find it to be anywhere "on time"

few notes, many poems
(the ideal state of affairs)

the unbelievable badness of the well-intentioned

"He could play a tomato can and make it sound good"
                                              —Red Rodney, on Charlie Parker

"signage"—buzzword at librarians' conference—means "to put up signs," like "No Eating"

"what happened between the time he wrote those *nice* poems. . . and. . ."

It's a *pulse* I'm after, one set up by cadenced phrases. Sometimes it goes on for a bit, sometimes it's over almost as soon as it began (Anton Webern's tiny pieces)—but then it changes, and changes again. Ted Berrigan used to say poets had a little guy in an office tucked away in their heads who "took care of things like meter."

On translation: The Latin *shrug* does *not* involve a raising of shoulders / contraction of shoulderblades. It is, instead, an oblique glance skyward, plus a tilt of chin, accompanied by palms outspread between waist and shoulder level: hence, "shrug" (noun or verb) is not really translatable into Spanish.

(Informant: Argentinian poet Mario Trejo)

A most succinct formulation of true 20th century aesthetic (and artist/ critic relationship):

> I
> put it down. You
> got to pick it up.

—Thelonious Sphere Monk,
quoted by David Meltzer
on p. 79 of *The Name: Selected Poetry 1973-1983*,
Black Sparrow, 1983

now doomed to write
elegies
until the end?

"If novels and poems fail to interest the Agora today, by the year 2091 such artifacts will not exist at all except as objects of monkish interest. This is neither a good nor a bad thing. It is simply not a famous thing."

—Gore Vidal,
Screening History (*New York Times Book Review*, 30 August 1992)

Translating the fragments of Hipponax: a "strange transmission"—or just the urge to get involved with some really *rowdy* dead guy?

Contemporary Canadians (thinking, here, of e.g. Gerry Gilbert, the late bp Nichol, others) seem both saner and more comprehensive in their work than most present U.S. poets (exceptions excepted)—they are not afraid to include much of what seems "dull," quotidian, "trivial"—they're more Greek—less Roman, less into Bread & Circuses, "special effects," or a striving for same. No more "substantial" than a good tune. I love it. & I really mean that.

What I'm most allergic to in poetry is the flowery earnestness that tries to convey an oh-aren't-we-all-in-this-together sort of feeling; that's worse, even, than vehement righteousness—because the latter, at least, is inherently funny in its indignation, anger being comical.

Another variety of earnestness implies that the author is an adept in some secret school of wisdom; it doesn't grate on me as much, but it does tend to put me to sleep.

Just think about it for a moment: Ezra Pound is funny, William Carlos Williams, Allen Ginsberg, Robert Creeley, Gregory Corso, Frank O'Hara are—not necessarily all the time, but frequently enough to make one put up with all their other delusions and pretensions.

"As we grow older, our nervous systems decelerate and our sense of *personal* time dawdles correspondingly. But *civil* time, of course, tramps on remorselessly, its divisions constant and inexorable. This is why our lives seem to pass more quickly as we age."
—William Boyd, *Brazzaville Beach*, p. 149

Pol Pot's "cultural revolutionists" *ate* their victims: the ultimate transgression, similar to practices of perverted "black magic" drug smuggler *santería* types; same desperate bag. . .The simulacrum of 'immortality' that kind of temporal power creates. The old Marquis nods and smiles: "Told you so. . .".

"I'm going to sit down and enjoy a really *empty* experience."

"The sonnet. . . is not a form at all but a state of mind. It is the extremely familiar dialogue upon which much writing is founded: a statement then a rejoinder of a sort, perhaps a reply, perhaps a variant of the the original—but a comeback of one sort or another."
—William Carlos Williams to James Laughlin,
Selected Letters, New York: W.W. Norton, 1989

"And what was it *like*, that *world* of yours?"

Thinking of the *bambini*. . .all the little rituals. . .past, lost, over in any case; but now we can't even wax sentimental over them.

treading
        the fine line
                between farce & pathos

why oh why did I spend eleven dollars on this tome in which two dead men *gibber* at each other? [Olson-Dahlberg correspondence]

"It is well known how Mary Magdalene came to Provençe to live after the Crucifixion, but less known that at Maximilien near Marseilles the tip of her nose used to be on view: no more than that because she had been cremated, but the tip of her nose remained imperishable because there Christ had kissed her."
> —E.S. Bates, *Touring in 1600*

"Myth—the practice of memory."
> —Joanne Kyger, in Naropa panel discussion, summer '93

"Almost any noun
is better alone than chaperoned
if it's the right noun, and very few
can stand two
adjectives. 'Unsettled dream' is
stronger than
'unsettled white dream'."

> —Ezra Pound to Parker Tyler, May '35
> in: Charles Boultenhouse, "Parker Tyler's Own Scandal,"
> *Film Culture* #77, Fall '92

"We are but older children, dear,
Who fret to find our bedtime near"
                          —Lewis Carroll to Alice

Benjamin Péret knew how to make a poem move *and* stand
absolutely still at the same time

when frozen water falls from the sky
we think of those who've said goodbye

"Confusion of voices as from several transmitters"
                                        —EP, Canto 72

who reads 100 poems writes like 100 poets
who reads 1,000 poems writes like herself

               —Ancient Chinese poet (?) via Gerry Gilbert
        via Joel Oppenheimer in *Poetry, the Ecology of the Soul*, p. 27

"Sometimes the only person who has devoted fifteen minutes of
mental receptivity and appreciation to a book, aside from its author
and (with luck) its publisher, is the cataloguer at the library who
described it for the O.C.L.C. database."
                          —Nicholson Baker, "Discards,"
                          in *The New Yorker*, April 4, '94

"Yours is not to complete
the work, but neither are you
free to abstain from it."
                    —Rabbi Tarphon, Pirkei Avot (2:21), via Joel Lewis

Take "American" (should be U.S.American!) poetry back from the
"English" Departments and give it to the readers we know are out
there—but who have grown tired of meekly browsing through yards
of identical-sounding narratives of resigned suburban existence.

Some of the young have always found satisfaction in prematurely
mummifying their elders, then painting the mummies in some
parodic fashion. And I suppose their elders, while still alive, have
always had a right to object to that practice.

"[I have] a lasting soft spot for the black banner of anarchy. My
innermost conviction is anarcho-syndicalist. Never mind that
I know it [= anarcho-syndicalism] can never be realized, but that is
where my secret love lies."
                    —Helmut Heissenbüttel (great German poet, d. 1996:
              for translations, see Rosmarie Waldrop, Michael Hamburger,
                                        Pierre Joris, & yrs truly)

"It's hard to say what unrealities may not enter the real, and there's as much in the spectrum from real to unreal as, say, between here or the zenith and the antipodes. [. . .] Man's bootstraps, his imagination, is quite a part of reality, or when that element fails, is unattained, or has no points of application, a stonier reality closes in, like death. [. . .] To be alive is to be chemically active—no ideas in a dead man's head— and the more points of interaction perceptions have with things in spaces other than that occupied by the head, or nowadays maybe the more they interact with such things, the faster they do, the greater [the] correspondence, correlation, cross-reference, then the truer they'll be."

—Larry Eigner (1927-1996), *areas / lights / heights*
ed. Benjamin Friedlander (p. 136)

Come to think of it, come to it early or late, language is pretty in-credible—not only in the sense of astounding, but also in the sense of unbelievable or hard to believe. Or so I believe. "Believe:" language and belief may be said to need each other. Belief, whether good bad or indifferent, requires language. It is, as we say, 'expressed in' lan-guage. I grew up (more or less, I suppose, and even somewhat agéd) in a time when some unbelievably bad beliefs generated some unbe-lievably bad language. The past tense employed in the previous sen-tence, while grammatically correct, is not *meant* to *mean* that the time to which I referred is over. Not by any *means*. Means, meaning, be-lief. The means we have to convey / signpost / describe meaning, and what we believe is 'meaningful,' are all contained in this overarching phenomenon called language whose creatures we ("humans") so sin-gularly are.

from Not a Form At All But a State of Mind

Sonnet IV

it is well known that Mary Magdalene came to Provençe
to live after the crucifixion
but less known that at Maximilien near Marseilles
the tip of her nose used to be on view

no more than that   because she had been cremated
but the tip of her nose remained imperishable
because there   the christ had kissed her
& who is going to pay   any attention to anything

when we aren't here anymore   "& what was it *like*
that *world* of yours?"   so much depends
on Fire Engine Number 5   myth is the practice of memory
dit Joanne Kyger

Johannes Kelpius first american composer
founded a commune called "the woman in the wilderness"

What Was It Like

(a remembrance of Allen Ginsberg's Howl*)*

—TO FIRST SET EYES on that small book—with a stark black and white typographical cover in a Charing Cross Road book shop of left-wing leanings in was it 1959? Twenty-five years old, an employee of the BBC's European Services in Bush House on the Strand, commuting there by double-decker bus from Camden Town, married, a few poems and a baby on the way—

No, no, let's not make this a 'personal memoir,' of the person by the person who was that person, who in the subsequent decade was to meet the person who was the author of that book, and so on and so forth—

But what was it, apart from all the obvious now legendary things, that made this reader perk up his mind-ears on first reading *Howl?*

That's a question impossible to answer with any claim to 'veracity,' after almost four decades of intervening existence. . .So this will be a collage, of matters remembered and matters to hand—such as the following text:

Heaven, Love, The Grave: cold potatoes.
We won't touch those. They've been
dealt with and well digested
by our civilization. What is new
is the question of syntax,
and it is urgent: Why do we
express
anything?
Why write poems or draw a girl
directly or as a mirror image?
Or doodle, on a hand's breadth of deckle-edged paper
countless plants, treetops, walls —

the latter, fat caterpillars with turtle heads
dragging themselves along, uncannily low
but definitely
composed?

Overwhelmingly
unanswerable!

It can't be in hopes of reward:
many die of starvation
in such endeavors. No: it is
an impulse
in the hand, remote-controlled,
by a layer of the brain,
a tardy messiah, perhaps, or a totem animal,
at the expense of content; a formal priapism.
It will pass.
But today,

syntax
is primary.

"The few who have recognized
some of it" (Goethe)
—of what, really?
Of syntax, I assume.

That is *Syntax* (my translation) by the German poet Gottfried Benn
(b.1886), published five years before his death in 1956—the year of
Howl's first publication.

. . .smashed phonograph records of nostalgic European
1930s German jazz. . . (*Howl*, p. 17)

According to Allen Ginsberg's own annotations to *Howl*, the line refers to recordings of Brecht/Weill musicals (*Howl: Original Draft. . . etc.* 128).

Benn, a contemporary of Brecht's (and, like William Carlos Williams, a physician-poet), spent the not-so-nostalgic European forties in "interior exile," his works banned and no publications allowed in Nazi Germany. An expressionist-realist in his beginnings, he later adopted a cool, sardonically formal stance reminiscent of Pound's *Mauberley*, but occasionally returned, as in *Syntax*, to the non-metrical cadenced verse of the early work.

By 1959, I had read some Benn in the original German but was not particularly attracted to it. It was cool, all right, but of a coolness that smacked of a Golden Ageism which made the reader suspect that this poet felt things had been much better in some distant, vaguely 'nobler' past. Brecht's work seemed to deal with the recent and far from noble past of the time leading up to and including World War II, and it did so with a witty and engagingly roguish 'outsider' air. But Benn's *Syntax* did herald a concern that resonated with post-WW II poets on both sides of the Atlantic: indeed, it was one of Allen Ginsberg's and Jack Kerouac's declared goals "to recreate the syntax and measure of poor human prose." (*Howl*, p. 20)

Authoritarian regimes, and the wars and conformist propaganda they generate, have a way of destroying large tracts of language on both the lexical and syntactical level.

Moloch the vast stone of war! Moloch the stunned
governments!. . . Moloch whose fingers are ten armies!
(*Howl*, p. 21)

Benn's compatriot Helmut Heissenbüttel (Ginsberg's senior by five years) who experienced "Moloch" very directly (like Blaise Cendrars in the world's previous great conflagration, he lost an arm in the trenches), had already responded to this call to recreate the syntax:

ceaselessly same faces meet in flow and counterflow
public address system speech uninterrupted
small girl's piano tunnels through the years
seagull's cry cuts dawn dream is still my sister
out of tunnels lit-up frontal surfaces appear
wood-fire skies of regions left behind
sidelined railroad cars doors open to November sun
smoke terrains stretched flat above marshaling yards
open grids of reflection in corrugated tin canals
landscape of canals and bridges
glittering parallel lines of the terrain before me
(Textbuch 1, 1954; my translation)

While Heissenbüttel seems to have received his version of Ginsberg's "sudden flash of the alchemy of the use of the ellipse the catalog the meter & the vibrating plane" (*Howl*, p. 19) at least in part from his post-WW II reading of Beckett, Joyce, and Stein, whose works were banned in Hitler's Reich—Ginsberg cites as his antecedents Christopher Smart ("derived from Hebrew Biblic prosody") and Guillaume Apollinaire ("montage of time & space, [. . .] compression of images, mind gaps or dissociations").

It may seem like an odd thing to do, this looking at more or less contemporary texts from 1950's Germany and the U.S. I have two excuses for it: 1) those were the two language spheres I still felt connected to in late fifties / early sixties London, after six years spent in Germany and Austria; 2) there were differences in these particular responses to a call for a new syntax—differences, I believe, generated by the relative distances from the epicenters of cultural meltdown.

In his introduction to the original edition of *Howl*, William Carlos Williams refers to "the life he [Ginsberg] had encountered about him during those first years after the *First* World War" (italics added). This slip of the pen indicates which one of the two wars had been the crucial experience for Williams. Later on in the introduction, Williams does refer to "that charnel house, *similar in every way* [! & italics added], to that of the Jews in the past war"—meaning the scenario of *Howl* and taking it as a documentary record of the author's experiences in "our own country, our own fondest purlieus". . .I recall being quite baffled by this, by the melodramatic reference to the "horrors he [AG] partakes of," and by the final "Hold back the edges of your gowns, Ladies, we are going through hell." Who were these capital-L "ladies?"

And if this was Hell, surely it was more of the order of Dante's or Villon's versions of it—where one encountered far more interesting and entertaining characters than in any heaven possible to imagine—than the one "of the Jews in the past war" Paul Celan memorialized in his great *Deathfugue* of 1945 (and practically all his poems thereafter).

Indeed—once past the grandiose (and oft-parodied) overstatement of *Howl*'s first line—if this was Hell, it sounded like so much FUN! It sounded like everything many, if not most, of those living in "our fondest purlieus" had missed out on—adventures and ecstasies and hangovers of the highest order. It was, in fact, a *student* poem, taking the same (as we are now fond of saying) 'transgressive' delight in stepping outside the boundaries of official bourgeois existence that the "poor scholar" François Villon—a witness, probably even participant of the first student riots at the University of Paris—shares with us in his *Legacy* and the *Ballad of Fat Margot*, penned five hundred years before.

In the weeks after Allen's death, "Beat" and other poetry-related Internet sites filled up with testimonials by persons now in their twenties, thirties, forties, saying how finding and reading *Howl* wherever they had happened to be, between the ages of twelve and twenty, in whatever oppressive circumstance they found themselves, had been "a lifesaver."

> Peyote solidities of halls, backyard green tree cemetery
> dawns, wine drunkenness over the rooftops,
> storefront boroughs of teahead joyride neon
> blinking traffic light, sun and moon and tree
> vibrations in the roaring winter dusks of Brook-
> lyn, ashcan rantings and kind king light of mind
> (*Howl*, p. 10.)

How that "teahead joyride neon blinking traffic light" leaps off the page again, just as it did forty years ago! In his annotations, Ginsberg conjectures that the "'teahead joyride' likely refers to drive Neal Cassady and Jack Kerouac took thru Brooklyn to hear some early-morning jazz late 1940s," and goes on to attribute the final "kind king light of mind" reference to a line of Kerouac's in *Mexico City Blues*. 1959 was the year of the first publication of those *Blues* by Grove Press and also of the first part of Kerouac's *Old Angel Midnight*, in Paul Carroll's *Big Table* out of Chicago:

> A long unlearned heavy school noises of piano legs in
> the smile paradise bed?
>
> (Old Angel Midnight, p. 39)

There it is, the same elliptical energy—generated by a syntax in which nouns telescope into each other, propelled by verbs so fast you can't see them; they aren't even "there."

Now and again, I find myself wishing that *all* of *Howl* proceeded like that—from "winter midnight streetlight smalltown rain" via "midnight solitude-bench dolmen-realms of love" back again to that marvelous "teahead joyride neon blinking traffic light". . .But such compression throughout the text would go against the romantic Anglophone antecedents the author honors: Shelley, Smart, and Whitman. Apollinaire's jump-cuts and ellipses are much quicker, and Kurt Schwitters (whose *Ursonate* is also cited among the precursors in the annotated edition) had of course moved on and out into sheer non-lexical mouth-music—which Ginsberg, with his keen sense and love of the historically outrageous, always seemed more capable of appreciating than many later homegrown versions of even innovative 'postmodern' writing. Whatever labels the critics may apply to *Howl* or later works, Ted Berrigan's comment made at The Naropa Institute's Jack Kerouac Conference in 1977 still rings true:

> Once *Howl* got known at all, everything was different.
> Something like that was never supposed to be able to
> exist and be a work of art, and—but once it did

exist, and was a work of art, it was a big work, a
major work.

(On the Level Everyday, p. 26)

But it is also true that there were other poems and books of poems I
read with great excitement back in those London days: they included
Charles Olson's *In Cold Hell, in Thicket* (1953), Robert Creeley's *The
Whip* (1957), Frank O'Hara's *Second Avenue* (1960) and *Biotherm* (1962)—
all of which presented a truly spectacular array of "recreations of the
syntax," or *syntaxes,* of American poetry. Donald M. Allen's anthology
The New American Poetry 1945-1960 gathered much of this, including
Howl, and much more in a volume that should never have been allowed
to go out of print: it is one of the Great American Classics of this cen-
tury. The youngsters in that book, of my exact generation (1934), are
Amiri Baraka (then LeRoi Jones), Ray Bremser, and John Wieners; others, like myself not included there but of the same live tradition, are
Ted Berrigan, Joseph Ceravolo, Diane di Prima, Robert Kelly, and
Joanne Kyger.

Terrific company.

As was Allen Ginsberg, our senior by eight years, the author of the
subject of this brief, rambling meditation—

> brave old lion
> gone out of reach now
> through the one door
> awaits us all

Works Cited

Gottfried Benn, "Syntax" (my translation): from Gottfried Benn, *Selected
Poems,* ed. F.W. Wodtke, London, Oxford University Press, 1970, p.105.

Ted Berrigan, *On the Level Everyday*, Jersey City, Talisman House, 1997, p. 26.

Paul Celan, "Deathfugue": many translations, most recently in John Felstiner, *Paul Celan, Poet, Survivor, Jew*, New Haven, Yale University Press, 1995, pp. 31-32.

Allen Ginsberg, "Howl" in: *Howl and Other Poems*, San Francisco, City Lights Books, 1956, pp. 9-28.

Allen Ginsberg, *Howl: Original Draft Facsimile, Transcript & Variant Versions, Fully Annotated by Author*, etc., ed. Barry Miles, New York, Harper & Row, 1986, pp. 125 & 175 ff.

Helmut Heissenbüttel, "Topographies (c)" (my translation), from: *Textbuch 1*, Olten, Walter Verlag, 1954, p. 9.

Jack Kerouac, *Mexico City Blues*, New York, Grove Press, 1959, p. 5.

Jack Kerouac, *Old Angel Midnight*, ed. Donald Allen, San Francisco, Grey Fox Press, 1993, p. 39.

Guillaume and Walt

ON APRIL FOOL S DAY, 1913, readers of the Parisian weekly *Mercure de France* ("The French Mercury") were treated to a remarkable "eyewitness account" of American poet Walt Whitman's funeral, twenty-one years after the event. It appeared in the weekly column penned by Guillaume Apollinaire, the great French poet, journalist, playwright, and promoter of the new century's new visual arts. This is what they read, under Apollinaire's byline:

WALT WHITMAN'S FUNERAL
AS DESCRIBED BY AN EYEWITNESS

The following detailed account of Walt Whitman's funeral was given to me by a participant. I took it down verbatim and have not added anything to it. This is, to my knowledge, the first detailed report ever published on this tremendously festive popular event.

"Walt Whitman, 'the good gray [poet],' had planned his own funeral ceremony. He had secretly saved up enough money to pay for a rather ugly mausoleum, undoubtedly of his own design, at the expense, I believe, of twenty thousand francs. After his death, his mourners rented a fairground mostly used by traveling circuses. The field was enclosed by a tall green fence. Three pavilions were built: one for Whitman's body lying in state; another for the barbecue (a popular American feast consisting of whole roasted cows and sheep); and a third for drinks: huge barrels of whiskey, beer, lemonade, and water.

"Three thousand five hundred people, men, women, and children, arrived at this funerary celebration. No formal invitations were required.

"All of this, it should be noted, took place near Camden (New Jersey).

"Music was provided by three big brass bands taking turns to play. Everybody Walt had ever known was there: poets, scholars, journalists from New York, politicians from Washington, old soldiers, war invalids from both the North and the South, farmers, oyster fishermen from his native county, stage drivers, drivers of Broadway's horse-drawn buses, Negroes, his old mistresses and *camerados* (a word he imagined was Spanish and used as a designation of the young men he had loved in his old age, never one to disguise his taste for philopedia), army surgeons, nurses male and female, parents of those wounded or killed in the war, all the people who had known Whitman and with whom he had corresponded.

"Pederasts had turned out *en masse*, the most admired among them a young man of twenty or twenty-two, celebrated for his looks, Peter Connelly, an Irish horse-car conductor in Washington and, later, Philadelphia, the one Whitman had loved the most.

"People were reminiscing how they had often seen Walt and Peter sitting on the curb eating slices of water melon.

"At this great party, or funeral ceremony, the public was also treated to great mounds of water melons.

"Speeches had not been scheduled in advance. Everyone was at liberty to speak whenever they were ready. Speakers simply climbed up on a chair or a table, and there were several orators in full flight at the same time.

"A great number of telegrams and cablegrams sent by the poets of America and Europe were read out loud.

"Several of these messages had been composed in verse.

"The majority of the harangues were addressed to Whitman's detractors.

"The free booze proved enormously popular with the assembled crowd. There were sixty fistfights, and the police arrested fifty persons.

"The party lasted from dawn to dusk. Several orators who made their speeches next to the casket punctuated their discourse by pounding the coffin lid with their fists.

"It was assumed, but not certain, that several of Whitman's children were among the guests, accompanied by their mothers, black or white.

"Whitman used to say that he had known six of his children but that he didn't doubt there were many others.

"At sundown a huge cortege formed with a ragtime band in the lead. Whitman's coffin followed, carried by six drunken pallbearers, and after it the crowd. The procession then moved from the fairground to the cemetery where Whitman's tomb stood on top of a hill. During the entire ceremony, the music never stopped.

"When it was time for the pallbearers to carry the coffin into the mausoleum, the door into it turned out to be too low, so the pallbearers went down on all fours: the coffin was then placed on their backs, and they carried it, crawling, into the tomb. Thus the greatest poet of democracy entered his final resting place, and the crowd, still singing, kissing and fondling, staggered off to the trolley-car station to return to Philadelphia."

Roger Shattuck, one of Apollinaire's distinguished translators and biographers (in *The Banquet Years*), comments that "[T]hrough the preceding fifteen years a group of admiring European critics had distorted Whitman's exotic figure beyond recognition." Among these admirers were Alfred Lord Tennyson and Algernon Swinburne in England and Arthur Rimbaud and Jules Laforgue in France, and Whitman had, through their good offices, attained a status somewhat similar to that of, say, Rumi in the contemporary U.S.—that of a great lovable exotic sage from far distant lands, a provider of optimistic antidotes to a threatened and threatening socioeconomic universe. "With this one facetious chronicle," Shattuck writes, "Apollinaire exploded the legend. The international polemic he provoked over Whitman's respectability and sexual mores spiced the pages of the *Mercure* for a year to come and tended to replace one misapprehension with another. Apollinaire coolly extricated himself from the free-for-all once it was well under way." As follows:

16 December 1913: CONCERNING WALT WHITMAN

My little article on Walt Whitman has met with an emotional reaction I did not anticipate.

I reported the details of Walt Whitman's funeral as they had been told to me in the presence of a young talented poet, M. Blaise Cendrars.

[Let me recommend Ron Padgett's wonderful translation of Cendrars' *Collected Poems*—AH.] I did not add or subtract anything from this account, believing that these were facts of common knowledge in America. Now that they have been contested, I regret my transmission of them. Unable to name a name that I am not at liberty to disclose, I ask you to dismiss the anecdote.

While the description of Whitman's self-designed tomb in the "eye-witness" piece is not entirely inaccurate, and the references to his sexual orientation, hotly contested at the time, seem relatively tame in the light of current research and mores, his actual funeral, while somewhat eccentric in its own way, was nothing like the celebratory orgy Apollinaire and Cendrars concocted. While there were ivy and laurel wreaths from some New York literati, there were no huge barrels of whiskey and beer, no fistfights, and probably not a great deal of public fondling and kissing. Whitman's lover, horse-car conductor Peter *Doyle*, not "Connelly" (to those French ears, one Irish name must have sounded as good as another) was nearly turned away from the door of the funeral parlor. At the mausoleum, Whitman's biographer Justin Kaplan tells us, there were "readings from Confucius, Buddha, Plato, the Koran, the Bible, and *Leaves of Grass*."

But in the poets' parallel universe, there remains the memory of the less high-toned, even farcical Utopian revels the readers of the *Mercure de France* vicariously enjoyed on April Fool's Day, 1913.

For The Naropa Institute's Whitman celebration 3 April 1997

Pentti Saarikoski and His Trilogy

THE TWENTY-FOURTH OF AUGUST 1998 marked the fifteenth anniversary of Pentti Saarikoski's departure from this planet, a week before his forty-sixth birthday. He left us twenty-two books of poems, six volumes of essayistic and autobiographical prose, three plays written for radio, a posthumous volume of diaries, and seventy booklength translations into Finnish from classical Greek, Latin, Italian, German, English, and Swedish, including Homer's Odyssey and James Joyce's *Ulysses*, the fragments of Heraclitus, Sappho's poems, Aristotle's Poetics, The Gospel According to St. Matthew, Francis Scott Fitzgerald's *Tender Is the Night*, works by Henry Miller, and J.D. Salinger's *Catcher in the Rye*. . .

A body of work of such dimensions, accomplished in such a relatively short lifetime, suggests a prodigy, a workaholic, probably an insomniac recluse hooked up to life-support systems in a guaranteed disturbance-free environment. Saarikoski certainly was both prodigious and prolific, but he recorded his dreams as important events in his life—so he must have slept—and in his twenties and thirties, far from being a recluse, was a highly visible actor in Finland's cultural political arena.

From the late nineteen-fifties through the early seventies, Saarikoski was a spokesman for what European historians now refer to as the Generation of '68. He was a highly literate and iconoclastic left-wing radical in a "buffer zone" country whose political climate in the Cold War years was one of far greater ambiguities than that of the major Western European states. He was, for a time, a youth idol—the popular press referred to him as "The Blond Beatle of the North"—whose often scandalous public behavior and pronouncements, combined with his introduction of uninhibited Finnish vernacular into the language of literature (particularly in his translations of *Ulysses* and *The Catcher in the Rye*), shocked many of his elders in much the same way that William S. Burroughs and Allen Ginsberg jolted the establishment in the United

States. The titles of some of his books from that period—*Out Loud; The Red Flags; I Look Out Over Stalin's Head*—indicate his search for a public and *engagé* mode of poetry. He became the editor of a literary and cultural journal sponsored by one of Finland's Marxist-Leninist parties but was relieved of that post after publishing the first-ever Finnish translations of Ezra Pound in the journal's inaugural issue. Herbert Lomas, the distinguished English poet and capable translator of Finnish poetry into British English, writes about first meeting Saarikoski around that time:

> "I remember him in a Helsinki bar in his early twenties, a confident young man with short black hair [so much for the 'blond Beatle' tag—AH] and a big grin, enjoying his fame, and drinking too much out of an apparently celebratory recklessness. He was changing everything." (1)

The Helsinki bar was, most likely, one called the *Kosmos*, where one may find, to this day, grizzled artists and writers who will reminisce about those nights with Pentti, with the typical humorously anguished Finnish nostalgia that has recently been brought to the movie screen by Aki Kaurismäki. To round out the picture, one should perhaps mention that Saarikoski was also married four times and fathered five children. His extended travels and sojourns as a guest of writers' organizations both East and West, commemorated in books titled *Walking Wherever*, *Letter to My Wife*, and *The Time in Prague*, did not do much for a stable family life in that hedonistic era.

The forty-two pages that launched Saarikoski into his time of fame and notoriety, in which he was "charting what it was like to be very much alive, Finnish but unparochial, and seriously preoccupied with a just and enlightened society in a time of world-wide confusion, unenlightenment and injustice" (Lomas) (2), were published in 1962 under the title *Mitä tapahtuu todella—What Is Really Going On.* (3)

I stress the number of *pages* because the page, as a unit, is an important element of that serial poem's composition. In its own way, the poem is as carefully and artfully composed, if not as hermetic, as Mallarmé's *A Throw of the Dice*. For a poem that became a kind of talisman for a

whole generation of young Finnish readers, it is, nevertheless, remark-
ably complex. It is not an inspired rant or catalogue propelled by a
rhetoric of outrage, like many of, say, Yevtushenko's or Ginsberg's works
of the same period. Reading Saarikoski's *What Is Really Going On* is
more like walking through a gallery with a series of white-washed rooms
and discovering, in each room, a verbal construct as limber-jointed and
changeable as an Alexander Calder mobile:

cold globules pass through the heart

        I want to get out from inside you
listen
      the trees
scratching against one another

light and warm in the cafe
       an absolute sign
     number or letter seen from a bus
         window every day

now I stand by the wall alone

and the disaster cannot be averted

----

hairs grow out of the star

      eye stuck to steaming asphalt

no one within the radius
     of this language
     went from the wood into the wood

                                    the end is near
                    the silver needles
dialectical materialism is
                        order and sense
                        of language and world

                    communications have been interrupted
                        the trees have stopped growing
                                    I stand on the sidewalk
not knowing my sex (4)

In an essay published in 1982, U.S.American critic Vincent B. Leitch
discusses *What Is Really Going On* as a—and perhaps the first—
"postmodern" Finnish poem. He points out that "Finnish literary historians make no formal distinction between modernist and
postmodernist modes—both of which arrived in Finnish-language poetry within a dozen years of one another. . ." (5) He goes on to quote
Saarikoski himself from an interview published shortly after the book:

> "I collected various sentences from newspapers, from
> people's speech, from books—anywhere, and then put
> together new units with them and my own sentences; I
> described my writing as 'democratic' or 'dialectical'
> because different notions were allowed to threaten one
> another in the work." (6)

My reason for discussing the 1962 book at such length in what is,
essentially, an introduction to *Trilogy* (Sun and Moon Press, Los Angeles, 1999), Saarikoski's last completed work, is simply that the former
can be seen as a kind of structural blueprint for the latter. I am tempted
to say that *What Is Really Going On* relates to *Trilogy* the way Kasimir
Malevich's early, lean, constructivist paintings relate to his mature work,
which may, in its figurativeness, seem "retro" to a superficial observer
while actually incorporating the conceptual principles and frames of
those early abstractions in a masterful way.

After a number of books in which Saarikoski explored versions of his earliest lyrical modes inspired by the Greek Anthology (whose Finnish translator he became), or the more didactic "Out Loud" form of discourse, he returned, in 1977—the publication year of the trilogy's first installment, *The Dance Floor on the Mountain*—to the "shifting magnetized field" (Leitch) of *What Is Really Going On*, and created a serial poem—not a poem sequence—of proportions comparable to the work of American counterparts such as Charles Olson, Paul Blackburn, Robin Blaser, and others. For a definition of "serial poem" I turn to Joseph M. Conte:

> "Narrative discourse endeavors to create the illusion of movement that is both linear and continuous. When we praise such writing for the progression of its terms toward some conclusion, we use such phrases as 'seamless logic' or 'smooth transition.' The movement of the serial poem, however, is curvilinear and disjunctive. It generates a centrifugal force, which is always directed away from a central axis [. . .] The series expresses its structure as a set of tangencies. Each contiguous part (or metonym) on the poetic line, aware of its antecedents and consequent links, implies a textual whole. But the intersection of these contexts will be small, and frequently they will meet only at discrete points." (7)

The great Anglo-Welsh poet David Jones describes his—probably still just "modern"?—sense of this kind of composition in the introductory note to his *Anathémata*:

> "What I have written has no plan, or at least is not planned. If it has a shape it is chiefly that it returns to its beginning. It has themes and a theme even if it wanders far. If it has a unity it is that what goes before conditions what comes after and *vice versa*. Rather as in a longish conversation between two friends, where one thing leads to another; but should a third party hear fragments of it, he might not know how the talk had passed from the cultivation of cabbages to Melchizedek, king of Salem. Though indeed he might guess." (8)

At the time of his work on *Trilogy*, the mid- to late seventies, Saarikoski had withdrawn from the limelight of Finnish public life and the strains two decades of being an only too enthusiastic big fish in a small pond had imposed on his mind and body. With his wife, Norwegian-Swedish writer Mia Berner, he established himself in an old house on an island just off the west coast of Sweden, not far from Gothenburg, and cultivated his own backyard in a typically troll-like way, superimposing the rich and various, wild and woolly landscape of his mind on the surrounding countryside with its low mountain ridges, petroglyphs, caves, and harbors. Lomas remembers meeting Saarikoski in this phase of his life:

"Shaggy, unkempt, with a *Kalevala* beard out of Gallén-Kallela, and a red dome of a cap that made him look like the priest of some arctic cult, there was nevertheless mischief in his eye. He knew that, as the physical incarnation of the mythical backwoods Finn, he represented a funny statement that he nevertheless took seriously. No one found the disguise more ridiculous than this free spirit himself. He had looked like the young Lorca; now he looked like a con-version of the ancient Väinämöinen." (9)

The not-too-distant exile from his homeland brought, as he himself observed, a renewed keenness to his poetry and prose, both in original work and translations. It also brought a sense of great changes continuing in the world, mostly not for what one might call "the better," and a concern for what a thinking and feeling person's stance might be when confronted by the implacability of historical forces this person had once, in the euphoric decade 1965-1975, dreamed of affecting by his life and work. Two untitled fragments from the early eighties bear witness to this:

I am the last
         human being
in the world
    I have survived
         the atomic war

IT IS NOT
THE TASK OF PHILOSOPHY
　　to change the world
　it is the World's task
　　　　to change philosophy
　And so I have become
　　　　　　a non-Marxist

Reading those lines, it strikes one as a genuinely Saarikoskian irony that their author was, not long before the time of writing them, invited to be a distinguished guest at the University of Iowa's International Writing Program—then *disinvited* because someone with that kind of veto power had 'discovered' Saarikoski's erstwhile "Communist" affiliations.

In *The Edge of Europe*, a book-length essay subtitled "a kinetic image" and written during the time of the trilogy's composition, Saarikoski returns to a philosopher who had been an inspiration to him in his teenage years: "Thinking of Kierkegaard. He wrote his doctoral dissertation on Socratic irony, and this should have provided a clue for the Kierkegaard scholars—but the only one who understood him correctly was Kafka, because for both Kafka and Kierkegaard life was a matter so serious that it could not be taken seriously." (10) In the trilogy, Saarikoski commemorates both great K's, as well as his mentor the pre-Socratic philosopher Heraclitus after whom the third volume of *Trilogy* is named: *The Dark One's Dances*. For the 1978 edition of his collected poems, Saarikoski wrote a footnote to a poem published in his very first book in 1958:

[the poem:]

The wise man, a Greek
called the Dark One
was right, I
see it now :

I'll never get there
by nightfall
and at night, asleep

I return to my
                                beginning (11)

[the footnote:]

"The wise man, a Greek:" the Dark One, Gr. *Skoteinos*,
nickname of the philosopher Heraclitus. Heraclitus is a
member of my poetry staff. (12)

In the introduction to his magnificently unadorned translation of
the Heraclitean fragments, Guy Davenport says, commenting on Frag-
ment 69:

"The Greek says that *ethos* is man's *daimon*; the moral climate of
a man's cultural complex (strictly, his psychological weather) is
what we mean when we say *daimon*, or guardian angel. [. . .] The
daimon has foresight, the *psyche* is blind and timebound. A thousand things happen to us daily which we sidestep or do not even
notice. We follow the events which we are characteristically
predisposed to co-operate with, designing what happens to us:
character is fate." (13)

In *Trilogy*, Saarikoski takes an extended, amused, bemused, and unpretentious look at some of the "thousand things" previously sidestepped
or unnoticed: the chores of dailiness, in a way often reminiscent of Paul
Blackburn's *Journals* (another great "last work"); his both familiar and
unfamiliar—northern but Swedish—surroundings; memories thought
long buried; the "Masks of God" he is reading about in Joseph Camp-
bell's three-volume work of that name, written—and read by Saarikoski—long before its author became a television personality. He also
wanders through the labyrinth of "events which we are characteristically

predisposed to co-operate with, designing what happens to us" and speculates that if we can transform *that* sign, the labyrinth, with its implications of rigidity and claustrophobia, into another, that of the dance, we may be able to revive an older, more truly participatory sense of both the word and the world.

There is, however, no dogmatism or "improving message" in these word-constructs, and in that respect, Saarikoski's trilogy differs from Olson's *Maximus* (or its great and antagonistic predecessor, the *Cantos*) and is closer in spirit to Robin Blaser's *The Holy Forest* and its erudite yet often disarmingly direct humor and wide range of attention. Of this particular phylum of United States poetry, Saarikoski, as far as we know, was familiar only with the *Cantos* and the work of William Carlos Williams, although I recall his mentioning an interest in Olson's work. The parallels with certain major serial poems written and published in the U.S. in the last three or four decades that Saarikoski's trilogy manifests are, it seems to me, due to a shared grounding in a) modernism—in Saarikoski's case, primarily via Pound and Joyce—and b) the ancient Greek poets and thinkers. "The most beautiful order of the world is still a random gathering of things insignificant in themselves," said Heraclitus; he also said that "the stuff of the psyche is a smoke-like substance of finest particles that gives rise to all other things; its particles are of less mass than any other substance, and it is constantly in motion: only movement can know movement." (14)

Saarikoski often spoke of his conviction that poetry and walking were closely related activities; he also said: "What I prefer to surround myself with is accidental, not intended, not premeditated, just left there, forgotten, lying around on the table—we'll use what comes to hand." (15) And: "The unexpected always happens, so unexpectedly that I have to pay attention every second: everything might suddenly shift into a new light. Nothing has changed, but everything's lit up differently." (16)

I have found his *Trilogy* a great book to leave lying around the house. Very often, when it has "come to hand," the way it witnesses the world's signs has shifted them into a new light, a light whose curious, even idiosyncratic *sanity* justifies his claim that Heraclitus is a "staff member" of his poetry. In life, Saarikoski often seemed to himself and others, not always happily, a brother from another planet; in his work, he made that planet worth a visit and a thoughtful stroll.

Notes

1   Herbert Lomas, "Haavikko and Saarikoski: Lyrical Strategies." In *2 PLUS 2: A Collection of International Writing*, ed. James Gill (Lausanne: Mylabris Press, 1985), p. 181.

2   Herbert Lomas, "Pentti Saarikoski" in *Contemporary Finnish Poetry*, ed. and trans. Herbert Lomas (Newcastle upon Tyne: Bloodaxe, 1991), p. 177.

3   Text from this volume is included in *Pentti Saarikoski, Poems 1958-1980*, ed. and trans. Anselm Hollo (West Branch, Iowa: Toothpaste Press, 1983), pp. 23-54. The selection is ten pages short of the complete volume: at the time, I found those ten pages either too "local" in their references to Finnish politics of the late fifties or otherwise redundant. Further readings of *What Is Really Going On* have convinced me that I was wrong, and I intend to finish a complete annotated translation of the book.

4   ibid., p. 30 and p. 33.

5   Vincent B. Leitch, "The Postmodern Poetry and Poetics of Pentti Saarikoski." *Scandinavian Review*, December 1982. p. 62.

6   ibid., p. 62.

7   Joseph M. Conte, *Unending Design: The Forms of Postmodern Poetry* (Ithaca and London: Cornell University Press, 1991), p. 23.

8   David Jones, *The Anathémata* (New York: The Viking Press, 1965), p. 33.

9   *2 PLUS 2*, p. 181.

10 Pentti Saarikoski, *Euroopan reuna. Kineettinen kuva* (*The Edge of Europe. A Kinetic Image*) (Helsinki: Otava Publishing Company, 1982), p. 172.

11 Pentti Saarikoski, *Runoja* (*Poems*) (Helsinki: Otava, 1958).

12 Pentti Saarikoski, *Tähänastiset runot* (*The Poems So Far*) (Helsinki: Otava, 1978).

13 *Herakleitos and Diogenes*, trans. from the Greek by Guy Davenport (San Francisco: Grey Fox Press, 1979), p. 9.

14 ibid., fragments 40 and 43, p. 18.

15 Pentti Saarikoski, *Asiaa tai ei* (*Something to Tell You, or Maybe Not*) (Helsinki: Otava, 1980). p. 64.

16 ibid., p. 126.

Gregorio the Herald

for Kyle Roderick

GREGORY CORSO'S PARTICULAR CHARM and poetic genius resides in his ability to incorporate bits of Elizabethan, Metaphysical, and Romantic (Keats, for sure, and Shelley, even more so) diction into poems of otherwise contemporary settings and concerns, and to do so not just decoratively but to get down to hardy perennial questions of the kind the Romantics dealt with—Biggies like beauty, death, power, fear, "meanings" of "life". And he *does* it—never pompous, always aware of paradox, with an effortless Mad Hatter sense of humor.

> *compact, dark, intense, alive with humorous ferocity*
> *walls of his London room*
> *covered with pictures of heroes —*
> *Rimbaud, Baudelaire, Poe*
> *curtains mostly drawn*
> *scratchy Hector Berlioz*
> *on very 'basic' record player*
>
> *(London, 1961)*

This may or may not have been after an evening at *Beyond the Fringe*, where we met Cyril Connolly, Peter Cook, and Dudley Moore—can't remember anything of consequence about that—and then proceeded to a Chelsea pub where Gregory was rebuffed by a young woman at the bar and stormed out, inveighing against "English cunts." We then reeled down the street to a small Indonesian restaurant, ordered and ate some incredibly hot food, and had more drinkies. Gregory was still ranting about the inability of English girls to perceive him as their savior, liberally lacing his sentences with "fucks" "shits" and "cunts", until a seven-foot Guardsman type (in civvies) appeared next to our table and sternly objected to such language, telling us that he had been enjoying a quiet dinner with a *lady*, etc., and offering to remove Gregory bodily from the premises if he didn't shut up pronto. Gregory then wanted to know if the Guardsman wanted to kill him and told him that if that was the case, he should please just go right ahead and *do* it. Two Bobbies then appeared on the scene with their classic "What seems to be the problem?" I told them Gregory was a renowned American poet, of a stature comparable to that of Dylan Thomas in the British Isles (come to think of it, perhaps not the best reference), and with Solomonic wisdom, the Bobbies decided that it was time for everyone to settle their reckonings and retire.

Gregory performed his duties as godfather impeccably. Josephine's mother, a devout South German Catholic, would have been heartbroken if our daughter Kaarina had not been properly received into the church. At the time, GC was, literally, the only Catholic we knew. When I asked him about it, he said sure, he'd be glad to, but the next day he told me he had checked out the baptismal liturgy, and among the lines the godparent had to speak was one he wasn't so sure about: "I renounce Satan and all his works. . ." After all, Satan. . . especially Milton's take on him. . . But after another day's reflection, he agreed to do it, and I remember his giving the priest a tip the size of which made the fellow's eyes bulge.

Ten (ye gods, it seemed like a hundred) years later, I attended a poetry conference chaired by Robert Vas Dias in Allendale, Michigan; Gregory was there among numerous other poets of our lineages—Paul Blackburn (the last summer of his life), Sonia Sanchez, Ted Berrigan, Jackson Mac Low, Robert Kelly, etc. etc. Paul chaired a session on "Sources," and Gregory pretended to have misunderstood the subject, saying he had thought it would be a discussion of the poets' favorite *sauces*.

Looking at *MINDFIELD* I find a kind of lucid loneliness in all of Gregory's work, and that does not seem to have changed over the years. Ranting, musing, or just talking, his poems don't "play to the gallery." They are too smart, too thoughtful, perhaps even *thought-ridden*, to lose an (if you wish) elitist sense of the poet as an aristocrat existing outside of, as well as in, his/her time. There are lines, even in the more rambling later works, that have the rock-hard humorous timelessness of Heraclitus or Diogenes. Indeed, there is a lot of Diogenes in Gregory.

Hearing him read in the summer of 1994, I was also—strangely, at first—reminded of Ezra Pound, his ear, his love of the word, his brilliant waywardness and contrariness. Gregory shares those traits and is capable of raising them to a level of subtle authority and delight.

Some Aereated Prose for a Panel on "Experimental Writing"

Anne Waldman: How do you go about constructing & conducting writing "experiments" (is there a point of reference)? Are there philosophical considerations?

AH: In an *experimental* culture,
based on the *experimental*,
secular, sociopolitical ideas
proposed by the French Revolution —
ideas which evolved
into the two dominant systems of this century:
one, socialism, two, capitalist democracy —
all art works
are bound to reflect that larger experimentalism,
by reactions ranging
from the participatory or complicitous
to the critical or rebellious.
Artists or not,
we are *surrounded* by those points of reference.
When the medium of the art is language,
as it is in writing,
we are also obliged to know
(in the sense of being aware of)
everything (or just about)
that language has been used for
in the past, in other cultures and civilizations.
This awareness may be employed
to decant contemporary subject matter
into old bottles (our "New Formalists,"
our "Cowboy and Cowgirl Poets")

—and who is to say that they
do not see their works as "experiments"?—
or it may lead to
the construction of new kinds of vehicles
or, simply, a new kind of nerve.

AW: Do you utilize experiments for the sheer technique?

AH: The short answer to this question is "No."
Since pedagogues at all levels
from grade school to Ph.D, programs
as well as your average book reviewers
still tend to classify all poetry
not written in textbook (or "old bottle") structures
as "experimental"
my own work has had that label tacked onto it.
As far as technique goes
I write things I'd like to read
and even read again. Years ago
a very bright younger student-poet
expressed surprise
tinged with some moral disapproval
at his discovery that almost none of my works
bore any classifiable textbook similarity to each other.
They came in bottles of all kinds of weird shapes & sizes.
The methods I use to make my poems
are various. I write lines,
I edit, I cut and paste, I rearrange;
I have incorporated into my writing
found / appropriated,
rearranged, otherwise altered, or re-contextualized
written material;
I try my best to get out from under
the ever-threatening Specters of the Obvious,
the Programmatic,
the Humorless,

the This-Will-Make-Me-Cringe-a-Decade-from-Now,
so that if there is any 'sheer technique' in my stuff
it's just *survival* technique,
get-it-out-there technique.
(Which is not say
those Specters haven't
caught up with me time & again
to drool and stomp on my Self-Esteem.)

AW: Are there concerns for "accessibility"? Should "methods" be known and understood?

AH: Some books
(and, yes, I am biased in favor of books)
some books are transparent ice cubes of amusing narrative
in what the French call the invisible style
and they can be terrific, like radio,
with the pictures much better than those on TV.
Some books are high-density constructs, thus more opaque,
and they, too, can be terrific, like *Ulysses*
or *Lunar Baedeker*
or unbelievably boring, like certain religious texts.
Those, I think, are the edges,
and most books exist somewhere inbetween.

I have always found the term "accessibility"
a little condescending: condescending both
to the book, and to its potential reader.
We now have "access" to more books
than any previous civilization.
We have more potential readers, too.
I trust readers
to become aware of the methods
they need to employ
to read what they find
and to have the desire to go on reading.

AW: Is there a "politics" of experimental writing?

AH: Historically, in this century,
"experimental" writing
has been associated with anti-authoritarian ideas.
In recent decades,
this anti-authoritarianism
has expressed itself in a rebellion against
the supreme authority of our civilization,
i.e., Corporate
increasingly non-democratic
Capital
and its built-in tendency
to turn each and every product
of the human brain
(or should I say
every product of a collaboration
between the human brain and the universe)
into a *commodity.*
In every realm of art,
the United States
(*not* the late Soviet Union!)
has created the best art for the masses—
that is,
the most commercially successful product for the masses —
the "masses" to be understood, here,
as masses of *consumers.*
It has also created a considerable amount of art
for an elite, or elites,
not necessarily defined by their wealth (which is power),
but by their high levels of
curiosity, eccentricity, and jadedness
—all of which I, personally, consider positive qualities.

Kerouac School summer session, 1 July 1996

Oh Didn't He Ramble
(Excerpts from the Informal Seminar Verbarium)

COLLAGE AND MONTAGE of various kinds are *major* modes of production. The Eisensteinian montage of Pound's *Cantos*, Tristan Tzara's words out of a grab-bag, Max Bense's "stochastic texts" and h.c. artmann's "verbariums," Gysin's and Burroughs's cut-ups, Jackson Mac Low's and Clark Coolidge's continued majestic oeuvres, Kathy Acker's montages and appropriations can all be seen as parts of the canon of modernist *and* postmodernist verbal imagination.

> "It is important to keep old hat
> in secret closet."
> —Ted Berrigan

It also seems important to connect with the reader. And for the reader, to connect with the author. Morty Sklar, co-editor (with the late lamented Darrell Gray) and publisher of *The Actualist Anthology* (Iowa City, 1966), states in his introduction to that book that "(E)ach Actualist is concerned with connecting with the reader on *some* level"—in retrospect, a concern charmingly optimistic in its assumption of a generalized "reader" who does not need to be thoroughly re-educated first, either in currently correct politico-literary theory, or in currently correct oppressed minority group allegiance, or in currently correct _____ (fill in the blank), before s/he can even presume to "connect" with the author.

Such an assumption may, of course, reflect a thoroughly antiquated bohemie-anarcho-individualist ideology, but I would not exchange it for another. Give me the Elysian, or Eleusinian, fields of poetry where Egil Skallagrimsson enjoys a picnic with Emily Dickinson, satyrs converse with cyborgs, and dinosaurs roam next to herds of programmed super-rabbits.

The spirit of the Iowa City Actualist group owed much to the work of Frank O'Hara and James Schuyler, and to the "actual" presence of Ted Berrigan in Iowa City for one memorable year. Ted composed his sonnets and odes with an immediacy, anarchic humor, and unpretentious artifice that still strike me as what might be The News.

It also occurs to me that O'Hara and Berrigan may well have been the last WASP poets *of the city*, and that the Actualists were aware of this. In the last two decades, the still-dominant WASP culture in the U.S. has devastated the great cities of its country, and the only poets left in them are known as the "marginalized."

When asked about the inspiration of his poems, Guillaume Apollinaire said: "Le plus souvent il s'agit de tristesse" ("It is mostly a question of sadness"). But, as he knew, the trick is to remember that *that* is absolutely *no* excuse to be *boring*, or *humorless*, or *too conveniently absent*. At the risk of pushing my Old Codger routine a bit too far, I have to say that much of what I read these days in our poetry periodicals and books strikes me as culpable of those three no-no's.

Many of those who believe they are upholding the great tradition from the Isles, or advocate a return to it after a—to their minds, rather regrettable—eighty-year excursion into what William Carlos Williams called "the American idiom," tend to be only too obviously (= boringly) 'present' in their work and solemn about it to boot, while some of those who still like to try on the old avant-garde hat often produce faintly ironic rearrangements of various debased public lingos that leave one neither amused (moved) nor entertained (smiling). The reason the irony is so faint is that there is, literally, nobody home. Which is very different from, say, Charles Olson's immersion in his best poems (e.g. "Maximus, from Dogtown"), or Louis Zukofsky metamorphosing into flowers of sound.

While the "mainstreamers" or proponents of the nostalgia esthetic rely too heavily on First Person Singular and First P. Singular's ancestors, relatives, lovers, enemies, pets and pet peeves, many of their seemingly more exploratory counterparts seem afflicted by the misconception that it is possible (or even desirable) to expunge all of the above, and all of one's feelings about (for and against) them, from the text. The currently sanctioned postmodern vanguard's main problem seems to be an infatuation with the not-so-new discovery of "opacity"—what we used to call "obscurity" in the old days, and not always pejoratively, either: Heraclitus was nicknamed "The Obscure" or Dark One. In present instances, this often seems to generate a kind of incoherent neo-Symbolism embedded in language that appears, well, *stunted*. It is true, as Philip Whalen has noted, that one cannot know what one "thinks" in a poem before one starts saying/writing it: but it is equally evident that there are times when one both thinks and writes rather less than memorably or communicatively, and if the results then seem opaque, that does not necessarily mean they are any good. Parenthetically, once again: I am aware of the interesting way in which the Mallarméan late Symbolist tradition is being revived by some contemporary French and American poets, but in some respects it feels too close to, or like another code for, the Anglo-Germano-Romantic strain. The reader should not have to "work to get the point" as if the text were a sophisticated MENSA exercise. With, say, John Ashbery, whom some may consider a sphinx, I get the sense that he is talking about exactly what he is talking about, not involving you in a "find-the-point" contest, nor nudging you to read his or his friends' latest essay on methodology (well, he couldn't do that, because they don't write those kinds of essays). . .

Hardly anyone writing and publishing poetry these days receives, or is ever likely to receive, any genuine—i.e., detailed, grounded, and thoughtful—"criticism." One of the reasons for this, pointed out by Samuel R. Delany in a 1974 essay, is simply that there is far too much of the stuff (in English, at least) for *anyone* to claim an "overview" of the "field."

Keep in mind that all of us have lived, are, and will be living through "interesting times"—times marked by unprecedented (and, as we are beginning to understand, insanely excessive) numbers of human beings on the planet, and therefore, and at least quantitatively speaking, also marked by unprecedented magnitudes of loss, injustice, oppression, and

Weltschmerz—"sorrow or sadness over the present or future woes of the world," says Webster's, and I would not leave out the *past* woes, either.

On (my) personal bias—important to declare: It seems to me that I have always been (not unpleasantly) "torn" between

> a) a poetry that is both transparent, or if you wish, limpid, and intelligent; that seems to be "saying itself": "My poetry is mainly just talk" —Ted Berrigan; that runs word-thought/word-feeling by me with economy and elegance, sometimes playing with different levels of available rhetoric, switching back and forth between them, and has some surprises in it the way good conversation does, often of a humorous nature—and

> b) the total Sargasso Sea of Signifiers, from Joyce to Stein to Bruce Andrews. I remember Ted telling me once that he cherished the works of his friends Aram Saroyan and Clark Coolidge "because they do my *research* for me."

In days not too long past when education always meant knowledge of at least one other language, mostly Latin, even people who did not necessarily consider themselves poets had a go at translating a bit of Catullus or Horace, merely for fun, as a mental and linguistic exercise. To some extent, in our Anglophone sphere, the great modernists of languages other than English have now taken the place of old Horace and Gaius Valerius: consider how many different translations there are of Baudelaire, Rimbaud, Apollinaire, Lorca, Neruda, even a poet as 'difficult' as Paul Celan.

The act of reading a poem with translation in mind is the *closest* reading imaginable, and that quality of attention, once acquired and exercised, is valuable in other contexts, not least in one's own writing. The participants in our translation workshops at The Kerouac School are practising writers, and the workshops give them an opportunity to make this kind of intensive study of texts by authors outside their linguistic realm—to get ideas, and to creatively understand, or misunderstand, what those people were up to.

It has been said that translation has no muse, but I think that it is presided over by a committee of at least six: Calliope (epic), Clio (history), Erato (lyric/amatory), Euterpe (music), Polyhymnia (sacred song), and Thalia (acting). The ancient Greeks were, of course, terrible chauvinists: they regarded other peoples (including their poets) who did not know and use *their* language as Barbarians, and translation was simply appropriation. I guess Ares presided over that. And when you find yourself truly engaged in a serious work of translation, it can indeed feel like an exhilarating form of Blake's "Mental Strife."

Let's Leave a Little Bark on This Log

in memoriam Joe Cardarelli

THE 26TH OF AUGUST, 1994, brought the sad news of the untimely death, at the age of fifty, of poet and painter Joe Cardarelli of Baltimore. Only a few days after Joe's return to the city from his summer residence in Maine, a heart attack cut him down. On the last day of his life, Joe supervised the installation of a show of his art works at the gallery of The Maryland Institute College of Art, including a large painted wood sculpture of a canoe. He had told me about this in a letter, saying it was to be a "decoy for bigger canoes in the sky". . . .

A graduate of the Johns Hopkins Writing Seminars, Joe Cardarelli taught poetry and writing at the Maryland Institute for twenty-seven years. During that tenure, he and the Institute were generous hosts to scores of writers and artists—Allen Ginsberg, Anne Waldman, Robert Creeley, Alice Notley, Ted Berrigan, Ntozake Shange, Edward Dorn, Joanne Kyger, Edward Sanders, to name but a few. Personally, I cannot imagine my two extended sojourns, and many subsequent short ones, in Baltimore without his presence as the hospitable guardian of the hearth of its poetry community.

The dedicatee of Sanders' *Hymn to Archilochus*, he shared with both author and subject of that poem their 2,700-year-old tradition of bardic utterance, and occasionally performed some of his works in collaborations with saxophonist Bob Gray. He was the author of numerous fugitive books and broadsides, including *phantom pod*, *From the Maine Book*, *The Milano Manifesto*, *Mouth of the Wolf*. The visiting poets' series Joe founded and directed at the Institute made the school one of the liveliest centers for poetry in the Baltimore-Washington D.C. area. His Black Mountain Poets' series in 1983/84 provided the material for a documentary video, *Black Mountain Revisited*, an effective montage of interviews and readings by Robert Duncan, Robert Creeley, Edward Dorn,

Joel Oppenheimer, and Jonathan Williams—in the case of Duncan and Oppenheimer, some of their last readings.

I first met Joe in 1970 when he came through Iowa City, but only got to know him well in 1975 when my peregrinations took me to Baltimore. We became close friends and remained in touch ever since.

Joe paid his first visit to Boulder and The Jack Kerouac School in April '94, when he and Lyn Hejinian gave a fiery and memorable reading in Shambhala Hall. Here is an excerpt from a poem he read that night, *The Unknown Story of Orpheus*:

> adrift in the bone boat pine hull   patched silk sails
> dim wind child a song among horned creatures
> tilted shaggy ears marooned in a waking dream
> knee deep in sand and foam and mused with grass
> long green stems strand from full red lips
> head lifted to catch airborne strains of midnight drummed
> as tho that cache were light in state arced across the lake

In the last letter I received from Joe, dated 6 August 1994, he refers to his work—with typical wry reticence—as "mixed comic philosophic rustic surrealism & sage quips. There must be something in there but I'm not sure what—indeterminate understated side images suspended around the clearing. Ah well." And the poem Joe contributed to Andrei Codrescu's and Laura Rosenthal's anthology *American Poets Say Goodbye to the Twentieth Century* (4 Walls 8 Windows, 1996) ends with the following lines:

> It's too bad sometimes I think
> too bad we can't see the air
> too bad the air's invisible
> too bad the air's not clearly there
> say as it is with just a little smoke
> we'd find ourselves new eyes
> taken up by the shapes of air tides
> the multi-layered, striated, tunneled
> twisted rolling wave shaped

moving patterns the air makes
no more or less substantial
than one hundred or thousand years.

That, indeed, is an integral part of what one sees/hears in Joe's poems: the "moving patterns the air makes," "suspended in the clearing." There are, of course, many "things" in that air—porcupines, canoes, mummified snakes metamorphosed into "Apollo Python," weather, lots of weather, friends and idols and family—brought onto the page in a language both consciously "unimproved" (let's leave a little bark on this log) yet delicate. To wander and alight in the clearings of his pages, to savor their blues (resignation + wisdom + humor) balanced by moments of almost archaic ecstasy (Sappho, Archilochus), was and still is a singular pleasure, time spent in "an actual dome-shield of frequencies / making all within hearing range secure." (A substantial selection of this work, *The Maine Book*, is slated for publication by Tropos Press, Baltimore.)

On Joe's second visit to Boulder, we drove up to Lookout Mountain, above Golden, and visited Col. William Frederick ("Buffalo Bill") Cody's grave. I had brought a little holy buffalo smoke for us to inhale upon that site, but there were too many youngsters and their parents around, so we didn't do it there & then.

So, only a few months later, Jane and I went to Baltimore, and I read my (inadequate, as they always are) *Words for Joe Cardarelli (Some of Which He Had Heard Before)*; David Hilton read a beautiful poem; Andrei Codrescu, David Franks, Roxie Powell, David Beaudouin, others also uttered words of grief and affection at the memorial service, which was quite festive, with a singer, a sax player, and a tall guy on the bagpipes; all of that followed by a big party, as Joe had always wished.

He loved poetry, and painting, and poets, and painters. He was a light in my life.

From a Letter
to Dawn Michelle Baude (1996)

Now, LET S SEE—what can I say that might be useful re: *Corvus?* It is, of course, my favorite book to date (being the most recent!), and my first with muchos *notes*—which of course don't always necessarily 'explain' anything unequivocally, but (I hope) give some indication of how this old mind works. . . .

Enclosed, recent issue of *New American Writing*, with ten-page contribution from a work I believe started with the final section of *Corvus*, the one titled *Survival Dancing*—as my note at the end of *How on Earth*—working title for the whole shot, if I ever finish it, now modified to *And How on Earth*, or *AHOE*—indicates.

The *AHOE* 'project' does, I think, hark back to *Blue Ceiling* and *Not a Form at All But a State of Mind*—both of which came about *alongside of* the other books-within-the-book (elegy for my sister (*1991*), the *Some Greeks* translations in tandem with *Hipponax*, and the *High Beam* poems). How to get back from the 14-line-box sequencing, fun as that was, to the looser cluster / constellation structures of *Ceiling*, but with less of a sense of the "laminated one-liners" (my term) feel of the latter? So, *Survival Dancing*, and on into *AHOE*. After reading Reverdy and Celan for 40-odd years, they may also be kicking in. As I told Alice Notley in a letter about this past summer session: "read with Pierre [Joris] and Anne [Waldman], thus the audience was treated to quite a range of accent & elocutionary virtuosity. Contrary, I think, to those two dear colleagues, I find it increasingly onerous to read those of my writings I fully understand, so didn't do that but read 22-part sequence of recent stuff where I can still feel happily at sea for most of the time."

In a brief intro to the reading, I said:

"What I'll read tonight consists of twenty-two short parts, separated (but not really *separated*) by lines that sound like titles but are more akin to silent movie captions. On occasion, as at a private viewing, I'll scroll back a little and amplify—not explain—what's going on."

Then I had a little epigraph composed for the occasion (don't know if it'll make it into later / final version):

> the poem
> a pattern of tea leaves
> on the bottom of the cup
>
> maybe Basho
> maybe Goethe

—an echo of Ed Sanders' "am I Goethe / or am I Schiller?"

Maybe also, in my graybeard days, feeling that there's no Diaghilev around any more to say: "Étonnez-moi!" (as he apparently kept telling Nijinsky)—or that I would now like to be my own Diaghilev.

Three Poets: a Review

Intimate Chronicles
by Christopher Middleton
(Riverdale-on-Hudson, NY: The Sheep Meadow Press, 1996)

Clean & Well Lit: Selected Poems 1987-1995
by Tom Raworth
(New York: Roof Books, 1996)

Selected Poems
by Douglas Oliver
(Jersey City, NJ: Talisman House, 1996)

> "both fortunate & un-
> —to have lived these past thirty years
> when so many delightful poets
> have been writing so many terrific poems:
> there was so much to read
> there wasn't much time left to write"

> —AH, in: *The Poet's Notebook*

—AND EVEN LESS TIME to come up with even semi-coherent responses to what there was to read! Plus, considering the complications involved in presuming to say anything at all about poetry at a time when discourse on the subject has become either theoreticized and specialized (in the journals), or generalized and purely gestural (in what passes for reviews in print media addressed to the public at large, such as the London and New York TLS's), a humble practitioner is bound to feel some trepidation 'daring' to 'review' three books of poetry of more than passing interest he was glad to find in 1996. May the following remarks be taken as made by one who has been "quite content to live on the Poets' Reservation" (Austrian poet Friederike Mayröcker, quoted on the jacket of her book *Notizen auf einem Kamel*, 1996), without any particular ambition to cross its borders into adjacent territories of discourse.

The back cover of Christopher Middleton's *Intimate Chronicles* quotes (genuine) "British critic T.J.C. Harris" as saying that "Middleton is one of the most extraordinary and extraordinarily neglected English poets." I wholeheartedly agree with the first half of that sentence. The second half, however, begs the question: neglected by whom? In my personal experience of *la vie littéraire* in London (1958 through 1967), what passed for official "recognition" then—in the pages of the *London Times Literary Supplement, Encounter, The London Magazine*, etc.—was still as biased in favor of a culturally 'genetic' stratum of poets as in Ezra Pound's early days there. Scanning the pages of Richard Caddel's lively UK poetry "listserve" on the World Wide Web (british-poets-request@mailbase.ac.uk), I can see that the situation really has not changed much in the past three decades: Last October, Iain Sinclair, the editor of *Conductors of Chaos*, a 488-page anthology of non-"mainstream" British poets, received the same dismissive-aggressive treatment in TLS pages as that meted out to Michael Horovitz for his *Children of Albion* back in 1970: "hideous extremes. . .charmless mannerism . . .gobbledygook. . . ." If it does not cleave to the post-Hardy/Frost/ Larkin line of wearily ironic pseudo-epiphany, it ain't what "we" think of as "poetry." Broadly speaking, it seems to be a matter of (mostly male) persons going to the same schools, then on to the same colleges, bonding against what used to be called "hearties" (= insensitive jocks), "discovering" the same lineages over and over again, and ending up in the ranks of reviewers for Establishment outlets. (1) The recent award of the Order of the British Empire to Liverpool stand-up comedian Roger McGough "for services to poetry" is only one more instance of the British Establishment's condescending and willfully obtuse view of the art.

In the early to mid-sixties, a pleasantly turbulent time in London, there were glimmerings of an opening up of that view in some quarters—due, in part, to an influx of U.S. visitors of the New American Poetry persuasion. Christopher Middleton's first mature collection, *torse 3* (Longmans, 1962) and Tom Raworth's *The Relation Ship* (Goliard,

1966) were major occasions of astonishment and delight at that time. Middleton's poetry of

> [. . .] a surface generated
> by a moving straight line
> which at every instant is turning,
> in some plane or other through it,
> about some point or other
> in its length

—from the OED definition that is the book's epigraph—was mercurial, erudite, playful, yet tough in ways far removed from either sour Larkinism or mod hipsterism. The poetic 'elsewheres' in *torse 3* certainly indicated a desire to leave behind such (then) dominant modes, but it was their diachronicity and courage in the face of post-WW II's terrible beauty that gave them their particular edge. Raworth's elliptical verbal cinematography, on the other hand, signaled an even more radical break with pastoral epiphanics, in its absolute lack of the self-consciousness that had still affected the work of otherwise notable maverick predecessors David Gascoyne and Philip O'Connor ("I can't *believe* I'm doing this, here in *England*") and still lingered in the work of contemporaries (among them Roger McGough, OBE).

Now it's thirty years later for all of us musketeers, and as Ted Berrigan was fond of noting, a year in a late twentieth century poet's life may easily equal ten in other cosmic time zones. . . The new work in Christopher Middleton's *Intimate Chronicles*, "'late work' by traditional measure" as the back cover notes, is strikingly youthful in the best sense: after a great many books of poems, essays, and brilliant translations of German poetry and prose, and thirty years spent teaching comparative literature in Austin, Texas, this poet's moves are, if anything, even faster and more precise:

UPON SAINT CRISPIN'S DAY

> Aha, said he,
>   Don't tell me you too

Keep somebody in mind,
    Who, when he squares,
On top of the heap now,
    His shoulders
To uncork
    Another wine bottle,
Holds his breath,
    Listens to the swish
Of arrows darkening
    The sky, and recalls
His forefather, the way
    He drew the longbow
At Agincourt.

Makes you shiver, eh? And then it makes you *question* that shiver. . . In the book, this is followed by a monologue in the persona of Paris ("Actually, folks, I am a stocky half-Hittite, / Dealer in used chariots and standard spears"), and then by one of the most stunning poems of the collection, "Ballad of the Putrefaction"—too long to quote here *in toto*, but here are a few lines, for a taste:

[. . .]
The poem of hateful persons hot in his mind
He met the girl whose work was to roll in creosote
Himself he wanted to set fire to the hateful persons
Nobodies governing nations without any sense of what's what
Not victors but victims of their spooks and greeds
[. . .]
Again he saw the squat bronze tractor woman
Straighten her headscarf in the hotel garden
Their monuments he murmured their long knives
Hack out the tongues of nightingale persons
Their slug fingers sign contracts for weapons
[. . .]

But again it is me the creosote girl who interrupts
We have escaped across many adjoining rooms
And arrive in a crypt where police wagons park
[. . .]
What if I doubt himself more deeply now than he can

Reminiscent of both Celan's *Todesfuge* and Notley's *The Descent of Alette*, this is one for the Great Inferno Anthology.

Intimate Chronicles insists on the poet's right to frame his or her work in whatever mode comes to hand—even, it seems, sometimes preferring the supposedly 'outdated' ones: travelogue, poem-"about"-music, poem-"about"-work of art, poem with classical reference, etc. As Middleton says in his essay "The Question of Novelty" (in *The Pursuit of the Kingfisher*, 1983):

Even in a relatively coherent society the levels of human reality intersect at odd angles and are stratified across loops and slopes. Those angles, loops and slopes are different warps of time in which people actually live, participating in the same epoch only tangentially and under sexual compulsion and economic coercion. [. . .]   Asynchronicity is the key, I am guessing, to any significant renewal, as act or event, personal or social [. . .] But it is altogether enigmatic, how the rare bird called 'new' can escape before being crushed, when the strata, enormous fluxions of time constantly solidifying into blocks, crash and grind against another."

In the "crash and grind" of our time, Christopher Middleton's subtle mind, ear, and eye do "stroke the living air, to make it hum." (*On a Photograph of Chekhov*).

Tom Raworth's *Clean & Well Lit: Selected Poems 1987—1995* is a most welcome companion volume to *Tottering State: Selected and New Poems 1963-1983* (The Figures, 1984) and *Eternal Sections* (Sun & Moon

Press, 1993). Driven by the "high speed submicroscopic / impetus" Middleton recognized early on in a poem dedicated to Raworth ("On Mozart's Birthday" in *The Lonely Suppers of W.V. Balloon*, 1975), these may well be the "fastest lines of the West," as Charles Bernstein has it; but no matter how fast they seem to be coming at you, their paratactic narrative is one that not only deserves but demands re-reading:

> [. . .]
> simply is no before
> slipping into gradual decline
> planets fall from a tree
> not to marry marks
> facing great uncertainties
> anxious to save money
> a half-explored land
> on the wrong trajectory
> hidden in mist
> where the outlines
> seemed broken puzzles
> gliding about the stage
> of an iris as it opened
> significance was yet to come
> [. . .]

As this fourteen-line excerpt from a ten-page poem ("Blue Screen") demonstrates, 'paratactic' does not quite describe what goes on here; 'meta-paratactic' might come closer. It is often impossible to know where one phrasal unit ends and the next one begins; the lines generate a spinning and spiraling progression through a scenery in motion—an effect created by quarrying intrinsically 'lazy' 'public' language, including that of the media, fragmenting and refracting this material, then combining it with what can also be read as 'private.'

There "simply is no before," or after, and "significance was"—still is, always—"yet to come." Individual lines retain their modular quality, which is (I think) to say that they might work just as well in reverse:

[. . .]
significance was yet to come
of an iris as it opened
gliding about the stage
seemed broken puzzles
where the outlines
hidden in mist
on the wrong trajectory
[. . .]

I once heard Raworth read another long poem ("Catacoustics" if memory serves) in line-by-line reverse from beginning to end. And the poem 'held up,' as they say: no problem. This curious modular *Sprechgesang* quality relates many of Raworth's poems to exploratory contemporary music in the Cage, Glass, and jazz traditions. "Out of a Sudden (Absence)," dedicated to the memory of Swiss-Italian poet Franco Beltrametti, graces the endpapers of this volume together with the music written for it by Steve Lacy. Its progression is representative of another, often submerged, strain of Raworth's poetry, the Shaker-like gift to be simple (not be confused with simplistic):

OUT OF A SUDDEN

the alphabet wonders
what it should do
paper feels useless
colours lose hue

while all musical notes
perform only in blue

a lombardy poplar
shadows the ground

drifted with swansdown
muffling the sound

at the tip of the lake
of the road to the south

above in the night sky
scattered by chance
stars cease their motion
poppies don't dance

in the grass standing still
by the path no-one walks

To my ear, this echoes and matches some of the finest of Samuel Beckett's French poems (particularly those Beckett himself did not put into English) or the work of Thomas A. Clark (a Scottish poet too little-known this side of the Atlantic); it strikes a note of genuinely modernist blues. The "he," too, in many of these poems, comes off as a classically 'modern' figure, shadowy yet considerably more present than personal pronouns (if any) in most contemporary work: "pretending he was a robot / respectable looking / legs hot and itchy. . . wandering among dogs / he is politely relieved of his wallet. . . he realised the image of a falling body / came from film / a slightly altered version. . ." ("Out of the Picture"). There is always a sense of *adventure*, not only in terms of concealed or fragmented narrative but also as an integral part of the stroboscopic and powerfully phanopoeic loops generated by the poems. And Raworth orchestrates all of this with stunning economy: these poems don't just *look* lean.

One of the epigraphs in the book is by Lord Byron: "But I have been familiar with ruins too long to dislike desolation." I don't doubt that the ruins to which Byron referred were not the decorative ones in Romantically landscaped gardens: with two hundred and fifty wars under its belt, *this* staggering century has surpassed Byron's in ruin production (those in Sarajevo are only the most obviously visible), and it is likely to create quite a few more before it vacates the stage to its grimly smiling successor. Raworth's poems, while fully conscious of what "a terminally depressed / board game" ("Emptily") the present 'world order' is, still celebrate the planet's ever odd beauty as perceived by the human brain:

> machines talk to themselves
> maintain a very persistent
> buzzing as the signal
> ends in a dramatic freeze
> close to the border
> on a street with a few orange trees

("The Vein")

In a preface to his *Selected Poems*, Douglas Oliver makes an important statement, important not only to his own work but in my opinion also to the total endeavor of poetry:

> "[But] the everyday lives of even the most brilliant
> among us have their simple and direct sides as well as
> philosophical, comic as well as tragic, romantic as well
> as classical, loving as well as satirical, baldly
> puzzled as well as cannily hermeneutic, cross-cultural
> as well as islanded-cultural. A poet's work might
> reflect that real variousness and avoid government by
> any persuasive definition of human consciousness or
> by any faddish narrowing of genres, forms or subject-
> matter. Without my claiming a cent for the results,
> that's what my own work tries to do."

The range implied by such a program is made manifest in this tightly packed selection from thirty years of brilliant, sturdy, quirky, always *concerned* work (in poetry as well as in fiction, essays, and the groundbreaking critical study *Poetry and Narrative in Performance*, 1989).

The politics of our historical circle of the Inferno, defined by "Western" corporate imperialism and Stalinist slave-stateism, are not apt to arouse poetic emotions to be recollected in tranquility: it takes a lifetime to find ways to deal with them, one's own complicity in them, and the sheer old Conradian horror of it all. Doug Oliver's way has been to re-consider, and rebuild, models of the epic, and the *Selected* contains a number of these works, either in their entirety (*The Diagram Poems, The Infant and the Pearl*) or in excerpts (*An Island That Is All the World, Penniless Politics, A Salvo for Africa*). *The Diagram Poems*, which take their subject matter from news reports on the Tupamaro rebellion in Uruguay, introduce visual elements into the text: literal diagrams, of an aspect both comical and threatening. *The Infant and the Pearl*, a tremendous response to what Thatcherism has wrought, "follows the prosody of the anonymous medieval classic, *Pearl*, with a few tricks to lighten it for the modern ear." *An Island. . .* alternates poems with moving prose passages of autobiography, and the more recent *Penniless Politics*, "a satire upon the world's most powerful nation whose voters just don't vote," and *A Salvo for Africa* combine various rhetorics of verse and prose. Recent shorter poems against the backdrop of Paris, where Oliver now lives, weave around the themes of individual and universal existence in a manner a little like an updated Apollinaire:

These thoughts in purple knots of cloud
dash down false lightning flashes like
neon signs above the glistening
Grands Boulevards, illuminating streetwise
melodramas not without beauty when
the will grows weary of the nightlong life
and you go walking.

("Well of Sorrows in Purple Tinctures")

It is, however, impossible to do Oliver's work justice by lifting brief quotes out of their context. The great pleasures it provides are embedded in what (especially after reading, say, Raworth) might seem a very leisurely kind of verbal progression: as in much of Bertolt Brecht's or

Edward Dorn's work, the words follow thoughts and perceptions emanating from an "I" that, while fully aware of being just another construct, examines and questions that construct in its experiential and existential passage. Thus, 'leisurely' does not cut it, at all: as Oliver notes in a prose passage excerpted from *An Island. . .*, "The gravity of a poem lies in its whole form [. . .] it is its ineffable nature." While this statement comes from a meditation on performance, it also describes the author's firm belief, evident throughout the work, that it is possible, still possible, as possible as ever, to represent one's world in terms that include overt ethical decisions and judgments—and that the work then becomes an autonomous extension of *who one is*, true to an intention that may be seen as larger and more inclusive than one "self." It occurs to me that if I were asked for a personal definition of "visionary," I would say that s/he is "one who participates in the thought of the world"—not going off into prescriptive Utopian imaginings or "systems," but engaging what s/he finds with the fullest possible range of intelligence and emotion at hand. In "Trink," a poem dedicated to Paul Celan's widow Gisèle Lestrange, Oliver salutes another Parisian exile, Heinrich Heine, with these affectionate lines:

> [. . .]
> remember, oh remember how he lay
> crippled on his eight-year grave and in his wine
> saw his young self drinking in a tavern
> mocking the pain in his spine; yet he never
> ceased his songs of "joy and fire" and wrote
> of Richard Lion-Heart riding in English forests,
> free from Austrian prisons.

And with that, I raise my glass of Apollinaris mineral water to these three walking forests of English, and wish them and their lucky readers many more years of The Work in The Life.

Notes

(1) There are, of course, parallel phenomena on the U.S. poetry rez: see, for instance, Dinitia Smith's attempt to classify the strains of contemporary American poetry in the *New York Times Sunday Magazine* ("The Poetry Pantheon," 19 February 1995). In her article, she labels Derek Walcott and Czeslaw Milosz "neo-Colonialists," calls Paul Hoover and Ann Lauterbach "Language Poets" and Philip Levine a "Magical Realist," and leaves one with the impression that all American poets of note are either members of quaint retro-Raj clubs in Manhattan or of gangs of raucous declamatory types hanging out in cafes in that same borough (with a few elders in retirement in Hawaii or Minnesota). Most of them are male. Women who cannot be squeezed into the "Earth Mothers" or "Sex, Gender, Politics" categories are simply off the map. In a country dumbed down by television, where "'poet' is almost as laughable a word as 'liberal'" (Jack Kroll in *Newsweek*, 1-9-95), this 'survey' merely reinforced sad stereotypes and made one suspect that the author's work as an "observer of poets" had not involved anything as retro as actually *reading* any poetry. Witness also Helen Vendler's recent dismissal of Mina Loy—no bad girls allowed in *this* canonical establishment.

From a Letter to Hoa Nguyen

[. . .] ALLEN GINSBERG S RECENT DEPARTURE from the corporeal domain has made me think about all those old questions again, in regard to the various 'hows' of poetry: how much (auto-) biographical freight poem-language can carry, and *how* it goes about doing so—Bob Grenier's notorious "I hate speech," back when, and Ted Berrigan's sense of poems just being stories with all the boring connective matter left out. Then again, what's boring to X may not be so to Y? The French (Royet-Journoud, Albiach) sense of near-autistic ("post-Mallarméan") little bursts of fragments—versus Alice Notley's and Ann Lauterbach's sense that poetry needs recognizable affect, a voice of emotion—how to navigate all that? "I" ask(s) "my" "self."

I'm sure 'group' and generational experience(s) play a big part in all of this: Charles Olson pointed out how anybody may "fall off the washing line" at some point—and then sit there with that sinking feeling of "I'm not understanding a word of this, even though I recognize all the letters" followed by "well, maybe I'm not *meant to*" followed by the closing of book or journal. [. . .]

On the Poem "le jazz hot"

LE JAZZ HOT

talked to my father again in a dream he seemed happy
perhaps a little older than the last time   told me
he had discovered something called '*le jazz hot*'
& found it of some interest

(1967)

IN THE YEARS immediately following my father's death (1967/8), I had
two vivid dreams in which he appeared. These four lines are a literal
transcription of one of them. The idea of a North European academic
of fairly conservative tastes posthumously "discovering" jazz struck me
as both funny and poignant. During my London sojourn in the sixties,
I DJ'ed a half-hour shortwave jazz program broadcast by the BBC's
Finnish Service; in it, I presented an anthology of the great American
art ranging from Sidney Bechet to Ornette Coleman (and was occasionally chided by my superiors for such eclecticism).

I cannot imagine a world without jazz, be it hot or cool. It is one of
the relatively few good reasons one has for enduring this century.

George Starbuck

—FIRST MET IN BUFFALO thirty years ago, during my first summer there in the company of himself, Ann London, Robert Creeley, John Logan, John Wieners, Arlene Ladden, Robert Hogg, Elaine Bowman, George Bowering, John Clarke, George Butterick, Albert Glover, Duncan McNaughton. . .A summer that definitely changed my life, as did George's subsequent invitation to come and teach at the Iowa Writers' Workshop, whose director he then was. *Cet ouvroir* was a very different place during his tenure from what it had been before, and, I believe, what it has been since. Not only did he invite Kathleen Fraser and her then husband Jack Marshall, he also invited Ted Berrigan, Steve Katz, Seymour Krim, David Ray—all, at that time, regarded as quite 'cutting edge' *makaris*, somewhat threatening, even, to the post-Paul Engle neo-Frostian/ pseudo-Williamsian 'Iowa' establishment.

George was a wit, an ironic master of traditional Anglo form, and a gentleman of wide and utterly non-provincial understanding of the art. I believe that he, Ted Berrigan, and your humble servant deserve credit in Poetry Heaven for our work in that place and time. Ted was politicked out of there after only one year, by the above mentioned establishmentarians; I outlasted George by a couple of years, thanks to Hans Breder of the visual arts department who fixed me up with an 'interdisciplinary' gig for a couple more years.

The roll call of 'our' (and, yes, Kathleen's & Jack's & Seymour's & Steve's) students looks pretty impressive today: Alice Notley, Robert Grenier, Ray DiPalma, Merrill Gilfillan, Michael Lally, Darrell Gray, Barrett Watten, Bob Perelman, Dave Morice. None of them, of course, quite as famous in the Old Iowa Lineage as a number of considerably dimmer lights who stayed on the confessional comfort track and reaped its rewards, such as they may have been.

So—Thank you, Captain George.

Ponge

Francis Ponge: Selected Poems
Edited by Margaret Guiton
Translated by Margaret Guiton, John Montague, & C.K. Williams
(Winston-Salem, Wake Forest University Press, 1994)

TWENTY-FIVE YEARS AGO, I bought a pocket-sized volume by Francis Ponge titled *Soap*, published in the excellent "Cape Editions" series edited by Nathaniel Tarn. Begun in the nineteen-forties, the original French—*Le Savon*—had appeared from Gallimard in 1967. Although less than ninety small pages, it felt like a *big* book—a galaxy of lectures, radio texts, speeches, journals, letters (including one from Albert Camus), and miniature plays, interspersed with repeated "Preludes" and concluding with five "Appendices". It was a book of constant interruptions, premeditated false starts, eccentric orbits around The Word and The Thing.

Ponge, who died in 1988 at the age of 89, is (with Larbaud, Michaux, de Dadelsen, others) one of the brilliant non-aligned non-"ists" among this century's French poets. In the introductory note to his section of translations in the present volume, poet John Montague tells us that

> [I]n French primary schools in the Third and Fourth
> Republic, there was an exercise called *leçons de*
> *choses*, Lessons in Things, in which an object,
> usually living—donkey or dandelion—is described
> both from a scientific and a literary point of view.
> The scientific was to suggest objectivity, the facts
> being those within range of a child, using
> *Larousse* or other general reference books,
> whereas the literary was subjective.

"Lessons in Things" was the form Francis Ponge appropriated, refined, and had a lot of fun with.

In his angry young man period, in the twenties, he had recognized the oppressiveness of human institutions and arrangements. He saw *language*, by which these perpetuate themselves, as the main instrument of that oppression. This is, of course, an active *meme* in much of twentieth century literature: it wants to destroy (Dada) or to deconstruct, and then somehow rebuild, verbal expression, making it resistant to, and a weapon of *résistance* against, the official version.

In 1926, Ponge proposed such a method: "an all-destroying flood of ill-chosen words" (Margaret Guiton, p. xi). *Très amusant*, that "ill-chosen", in its tacit acknowledgment of a dominant discourse. . . Four years later, he wrote that it was "not a question of cleaning the Augean stable but painting the walls with its own shit." Antonin Artaud would proceed to do precisely that.

The solution Ponge eventually found and made his own was both simpler and more complicated. It consisted of going back to the most basic of French forms, retaining and mocking its pedantic formality, pushing its envelope, filling it with helium, nitrous oxide, and the occasional whiff of vinegar:

> Tired of holding back all winter long, the trees
> suddenly feel they've been had. They can't stand
> it any more: they release their verbiage, a flood,
> a vomit of green. They try to achieve a complete
> foliage of verbiage. So what? Let it sort itself
> out as it can. And, in fact, it *does.* There's no
> such thing as random foliation. . . .
>   ("The Cycle of Seasons," C.K. Williams trl.)

"Taking the side of things" (the title of one of his books), Ponge uses ironic-affectionate contemplation of objects, ranging from "The Candle" to "Dung" to "The New Spider," to etymologize and analogize, and finally, to comment on the human (language) universe and our notions of what that might be.

In the introduction to her translation of Ponge's *The Making of the Pré* (1979), Lee Fahnestock writes:

For many years Ponge has affirmed that the world, full of natural autonomous objects, must exist. Words, too, are objects that impinge on the senses, demand notice, provoke affection or disgust, revealing to the adept the lesson of their power. [. . .] Successive meanings, for Ponge, give words their *épaisseur*, a physical density, but particularly a semantic depth. [. . .] Once they are recognized as different from their names, objects and words must be freshly coupled.

The classically French pedantry of Ponge's method is so effortless it's relaxing. Despite its frequent associative leaps, puns, and pirouettes, his poetry does not seem 'difficult' or self-indulgent:

> This varnished box shows nothing that protrudes, only a
> knob to turn to the next click, that quite soon many
> little aluminum skyscrapers light up weakly within,
> while savage shoutings spurt contending for our
> attention. A little apparatus with a wonderful
> 'selectivity'. Ah, how ingenious it is to have
> refined the ear to this point. Why? To pour into it
> incessantly the most outrageous vulgarities.
> (From "The Radio", trl. John Montague)

A note on Ponge in Paul Auster's magnificent *Random House Book of Twentieth-Century French Poetry* (New York, 1982) lists the following English translations of his work: *Soap*, trans. by Lane Dunlop (Jonathan Cape, 1969); *The Voice of Things*, trans. by Beth Archer (McGraw-Hill) and *Things*, trans. by Cid Corman (Grossman), both 1971; *The Sun Placed in the Abyss*, trans. by Serge Gavronsky (U of California Press, 1979). To these should be added *The Making of the* Pré, translated by Lee Fahnestock (U of Missouri Press, 1979). It is both typical and regrettable that Wake Forest's *Selected* does not include any of these translators' work. I am not familiar with Archer's and Gavronsky's books, but both Corman and Dunlop, as well as Peter Riley and Richard Wilbur (in Auster's anthology) have done well by Ponge. Fahnestock's *The Making of the* Pré (Fr. *pré*—meadow) is a beautifully produced book of facsimiles of drafts leading to a seven-page 'finished' poem at the end of which M. Ponge literally puts himself under the sod. The book—probably remaindered by now—also includes full-color reproductions of the maps, drawings, photographs and paintings that contributed to its making.

Pleasing as it is to a polyglot reader, the bilingual *en face* format of Wake Forest's *Selected* is ultimately academic in the negative sense—being too timid to acknowledge French poetry translated by U.S.American poets as (for better or worse) an integral part of U.S.American literature. Most poets and readers of poetry would be willing to sacrifice that format in favor of a bigger book of texts in English (for instance, one that included *Soap*). That said, it strikes me as a lack of *academic* decorum that the Ponge volume, though annotated, does not provide the reader with bibliographies of a) original publications and b) translations into English.

How as they say ever, it is a pleasure to have this *Selected*: may it lead present-day readers to the cranky sage with the steely twinkle in his eye.

Lighten Up

Mao & Matisse
Poems by Ed Friedman
(Hanging Loose Press, 1995)

THERE ARE BOOKS ONE IS GLAD to have on the shelf when the outside world's news darken the skies inside the cabeza. For this writer, Ed Friedman's *Humans Work* (Helpful Books, 1988) has long been one of those libros. And whenever vapors of Gibran or Bly or one of Rumi's innumerable translators threaten to invade workshop discourse, I exorcise them with the *Translate into Arabic* sequence—e.g., *Prophecy:*

> A pair of dark eyes watch me through a bullet hole in the cantina.
> I know it's the Prophet himself in a $50 black stetson.
> HOW do I know? Heh heh heh.
> I feel mighty fine.

Now *Mao & Matisse* joins its predecessor on that shelf, and it is likewise a joy. Ron Padgett's blurb is one of the sharpest recent examples of the mini-essayistic form:

> It's as if the poems [. . .] were written by several people whose second language is a floaty, slightly dislocated, and thoroughly amusing English, from which there emerges a new lyricism that provides a rarity these days: pure pleasure.

By all ye gods and demons, we can use THAT! In MEGA-doses! As an antidote to both media spew and the product of practitioners who try very hard to sound either 1) like just one and indivisible marvelously 'integrated' 'person' or 2) like the recipient of a genetically enhanced insect brain transplant. Master of notes and tones, Ed pleases the inner ("Étonnez-moi!") Diaghilev:

> [. . .] You appraise me with blue vacant eyes
> Very shallow, very wide
> Nothing stands still for two-toned shirts
> That mirror the design of your car radio
> Why even my well-practiced blank expression
> Dissolves at the mention of fresh grazing
> I am Mr. Cow now and Mrs. Free-swimming Jellyfish
> Undulating across the tangerine linoleum
> Petroglyphs verify our continued grooming

Some of the shorter poems bring to mind Blaise Cendrars' great *Kodak* or *Elastic* works:

> *The Strongman Act*
>
> Six coding stations with pre-distributors
> Relay a response
> To the mother of my children
> Say all you know
> Without reserve
> As often as necessary
> Well-chosen anecdotes
> Enhance theory and
> Develop a fully cultured acumen

The longer ones (*Living Under, November, Presence*) proceed in an open form syntax that manifests delight in thought, perception, and the next-to-each-otherness of words:

> Mariachi on a mule
> negotiates boulders and cacti.

A melodious tune circle
spins in the vista.

Hasta la vista.
Vive la France!

("Living Under")

Shifting and swerving through the mind's traffic, Ed Friedman's works reflect a poetics of hope: Hope for the idiom's ability to cope; hope for the continued lope of humans through their perennially terrifying and hilarious environment; hope for others out there to stop moping and start troping in similar keys.

There is evidence of the existence of some younger ones "out there" working to restore a non-insectoid sense of humor to American poetry, in the great (non-provincial) New York School tradition: Kevin Opstedal of San Francisco and Joel Dailey of New Orleans come to mind. The Establishment (yes, Virginia, we do have one in these States) will of course go on ignoring anything that seems the least bit fun, always preferring a Paul Muldoon's bleakly twisted and overdetermined 'wit' to Ted, or Anselm, or Edmund Berrigan's genuine article. Or to this lovely work, Ed Friedman's *Mao & Matisse*. I notice that I have started making a short list for an anthology: What to call it? So many of the poems in our recent mudslide of anthologies of contemporary versos are dismally humorless. Perhaps *The Blown Ones*, the title of the book's final (prose) poem, would serve as a title, and Ed should be the Ed.:

[. . .] Write about us in those impressive alphabets designed during the period of Russian Constructivism. Busby Berkeley will provide movement, a waterfall, a bride, telephone operators at their switchboards. There's a collection here forming. Notice the ducks.

Quixotic Unanswered Letter
to a Poet / Book Reviewer
of the New York Times

24 August 1994

DEAR *******:

I've been meaning to write to you ever since I read your kind words on my translation, in your review of **** *****' novel in the NY Times Book Review. So, first of all, many thanks! It is rare for a literary translator of contemporary works to receive any mention—except when she or he has blundered in ways that provide entertaining column inches. . .

Three cheers, likewise, for your review of Zbigniew Herbert, John Montague, and Michael Krüger, in last Sunday's NYTBR. I too have been a staunch fan of Herbert's ever since I read him in German translations in the late Fifties, and spent a pleasant afternoon with him at an early seventies literary conference, in the company of Czeslaw Milosz and George Kimball III (then still a poet and classy pornographer, now noted Bóston sportswriter). You are absolutely right in saying that in a "just world" Herbert would have received a Nobel Prize long ago; then again, in a "just world" a "Nobel Prize" probably wouldn't exist. And, parenthetically, in such a Utopia, books by some pretty good poets like Alice Notley, Bernadette Mayer, Edward Dorn, Tom Clark, Ron Padgett, Tom Raworth, perhaps even myself? would occasionally be noticed in the pages of the NYTBR.

I also agree with the first two sentences of your review: "Post-modernism has been a rocky road for poets. It is hard to mix emotion and sincerity with irony and distance." Then, however, I find myself bristling at: "the rejection of sense and emotion by the Language poets. . . ."

It is one thing to say that the "New Formalists" are "nostalgic"—nostalgia is, after all, quite fashionable and thus forgivable (perhaps even charming and attractive). But to say that "Language poets" reject, hence, lack, both "sense and emotion," is a different matter. It reinforces prejudices that have been bandied about far too long, in the pages of the New York Times Book Review and in certain more academically oriented publications.

While I agree that there are writers counted among the Languageists whose work is of such intentional opacity that it may fit better into your third category—those who "retreat to simple obfuscation"—I feel obliged to point out (and urge you to read) the works of e.g. Carla Harryman, Robert Grenier, Lyn Hejinian, Charles Bernstein, Leslie Scalapino, and Bob Perelman, and to find, I believe, plenty of "sense and emotion" in them. Grenier's and Hejinian's poems share much of the concern and integrity we love in Herbert's work, even though their late-century American rhetorics differ from his (as they should). Scalapino, to my mind, is *the* American poet of Anxiety writ large (truly large, far beyond a Plath's or Sexton's pop-psych insistences), and Perelman is one of the few capable of writing a genuine political poem, i.e., one that does not resort to finger-pointing, special pleading, or plain decibels.

I realize that my feelings about this have to do with the unprecedented proliferation and concurrent "ghettoization" of American poetry in the last thirty years, which have made it impossible for anyone to claim an "overview" of the "field." Nevertheless, it is one's duty to protest, however vainly, against the onrolling wave of Philistine ignorance that will prove as revisionist (but perhaps not as revocable) as Stalinist history-writing ever was.

Yours, etc.

Anselm Hollo
1934—

1

The Way

The way you got to be the way you were
just a moment ago

is the way of "the moment"
a big old notion in which you can never

find yourself
so stagger on on your quest

for the other big old notion
"the now"

as in *right now*
as you just were right then (1)

What do I *know* of my beginning(s)? What does *anyone* really know about theirs?

What will generations whose earliest moments have been recorded, on film or videotape, learn from those images and sounds when they review them later in life? What "was it all about?"

What if one recorded every waking (and possibly even sleeping) moment of one's life up to, say, thirty-five, and then spent one's remaining years watching the tape?

A recent study (2) suggests that each mental replay of a memory is more like a re-*make*, a re-interpretation, whose materials are fragmentary and in far from 'archival' condition:

maternity home with
big black bronze
statue of sheepdog
in front who
knows the connection
but as we
walk past someone
points at it
says that is
where you were
born
that someone
quite possibly my (3)

—well, mother, most likely. . .I remember writing those purposefully halting lines (an interlude in a longish and otherwise fairly flowing sequence, *Lunch in Fur*), trying to deal with the horrors and joys of seemingly interminable midlife crises, one bitter cold winter night in a rented trailer in Cottonwood, Minnesota; but I cannot state with any certainty whether they originated in a dream or in my 'waking' memory. Walking around the tall cliffs and boulders of Kaivopuisto (a Helsinki city park overlooking the old harbor) not too long ago, I was unable to locate the small private maternity hospital (possibly called "Salus"—?) there, nor the big bronze dog (of the breed known as "German Shepherd" in the U.S. and "Alsatian" in the U.K.). Nor do I have a clear idea why such a sculptural guard should grace the entrance of a place where human children are born. . .

In any case, my birth certificate states that I was born in that city, on the twelfth of April, 1934, the son of Juho August Hollo (1885-1967), professor of pedagogy (educational theory) at the University of Helsinki and translator of world literature from fourteen languages into Finnish, and Iris Antonina Anna Walden (1899-1983), music teacher and translator of scholarly (mostly ethnographic) texts into German.

Juho, or "J.A. Hollo" as he signed himself, was a native of the town of Laihia in the province of Ostrobothnia, the firstborn son of a

Finnish master cabinet maker and his Swedish wife. Iris was born in Riga, Latvia. Her mother was a "von" from an originally Prussian family, her father a Baltic German scientist and professor of organic chemistry. She met J.A. in Leipzig, Germany, where she was studying music and he was doing postgraduate work. They married and went to live in Vienna, where my sister Irina (1921-1991) was born. They returned to Helsinki in the late twenties.

While my mother's background was urban (Riga, St. Petersburg, Moscow), my father's family weren't exactly country bumpkins: my paternal grandfather, who ended up owning a furniture factory, was an avid reader and had at least one close friend who was a writer, the novelist Santeri Alkio. According to family legend, this grandfather once became so enthused by the classics that he tried (in vain) to persuade his womenfolk to wear Greek garb while going about their domestic chores—in the summer, presumably, since the climate would have made this rather impractical during the rest of the year. The classics continued to loom large in our family history: his eldest son, my father, translated Plato, and my father's closest friend was the poet Otto Manninen who first performed the *Iliad* and the *Odyssey* in Finnish. A couple of years ago I, a mere midget in the field, completed an American English version of the fragments of Hipponax.

When I was five, my mother took me to visit her parents in Rostock, Germany, where grandfather Paul Walden (1863-1957) was then teaching, and on to Berlin. I recall a ride down a wide nocturnal avenue, black and glittering with rain, which must have been the Kurfürstendamm; a walk past the Reichskanzlei, Hitler's headquarters, and its stone-faced sentries; a magical, "Old Dutch interior" kind of evening with my godfather, Robert Fellinger, and his Wendish housekeeper "Tante Helene"—one of the few survivors of her tribe, and, as I heard later, a life-long opium user. (Her people, also known as the Lusatian Sorbs, are the smallest Slavonic group without a country of their own.) Portly and maternal, she radiated an old-world kindness and sweetness that I did not, at that time, encounter in my grandparents' home. They considered me a "difficult" child, and I remember overhearing conversation in which grandma Wanda von Lutzau exhorted my mother, in typical Victorian / Wilhelminian fashion, to "break his will."

I never really knew my paternal grandparents. I must have been very young on the one visit to Laihia we made while they were still alive. I remember a large, bearded patriarch in a rocking chair, and the thumb on his right hand, which had been sliced off at the first joint in some long-ago woodworking accident. My father's mother is an even fuzzier snapshot of a busy little woman wearing a crocheted black shawl with fringes. . .This visit, too, must have taken place just before the second great slaughter of the century began.

Helsinki, 1940

Exploding, shattering, burning

Big lights in the sky

& this was
Heaven's Gate?

No no it's just the front door
same old front door you know from the daytime
& we're just waiting for a lull in the action
to cross the yard, get down to the shelter
& meet the folks, all the other folks
from all the other apartments

& there was a young woman
at least ten years older
he thought very beautiful

Blankets & wooden beams & crackling radios & chatter

It was better than heaven, it was
being safe in the earth, surrounded by many

all of whom really felt like living (4)

In order to improve our chances of survival, my parents, my sister, and I packed our bags and took the steamer across the Gulf of Bothnia to Stockholm, where we stayed long enough for me to learn to read, and to learn Swedish at the same time. Until then, I had spoken only the main conversational language of my family, which was German. My sister Irina grew tired of reading and translating the Swedish speech-balloons in my favorite comics (*Felix the Cat*, *Mandrake the Magician*, *Nancy & Sluggo*, *The Phantom*) in the back pages of the Stockholm dailies, so she obtained a Swedish ABC book and proceeded to teach me to read. In Swedish. When we returned to Helsinki, my father taught me Finnish in a couple of months, preparing me for Miss Ojansuu's elementary school just around the corner from where we lived. Our home was on the second floor of a large apartment building on Mariankatu in the Old Town of Helsinki; the apartment had twelve-foot ceilings and large white Dutch tile stoves, heated with wood fetched up from the cellar and stored in a large box in the kitchen.

> grew up in finland
> the south of that land
>
> father philosophos & writer
> wrote the works of cervantes in finnish
>
> mother a talker & talker
> all over the known world
>
> but really my parents
> you were giant white rabbit people
> very wealthy & powerful
> lived in a palace place
> under elephant rock
>
> thrones
> robes
> & a great golden light
> strobed out from behind them (5)

With a sister thirteen years older, I grew up much like an only child, one who was born into a family that was in many not always tangible ways one of "exiles." My father, the eldest of six, had left the rural province of his birth for the cities and academic life as a young man, and had renounced his share in the family business in favor of his siblings. My mother, a Balt born in Riga, whose German ancestors had colonized Latvia hundreds of years ago, and who had been raised in Czarist Russia and Weimar Germany, never really felt at home in Finland—even though it, too, is a Baltic region. I have reason to believe that she sometimes told herself she was living among barbarians. Her relations with my father's family were, however, mostly cordial, and much of the culture shock she had initially suffered had worn off by the time I appeared on the scene.

> when my mother was but a young lass from germany, moved
> to finland for a life with my (then, future) father, they were in-
> vited to dinner, a formal academic occasion, & she was seated
> next to a dignitary chosen for his command of spoken german. it
> was a long dinner, with many speeches, given in finnish, an ugric
> language my mother did not understand. the only attempt at con-
> versation her neighbor-at-table managed was the statement: "this
> is good pig, is it not" (in german, of course). she is still fond of
> the story, fifty years later. (6)

Finns are, of course, notorious for being taciturn. The hot young Finnish *auteur* of recent years, Aki Kaurismäki of *Leningrad Cowboys* fame, puts that trait to good satirical use in his film *The Match Factory Girl*: in terms of the spoken word, its script could have been written by a newt. My mother, on the other hand, was indeed "a talker and talker / all over the known world," and I think one reason why my sister Irina never left the nest until dear Amy (our nickname for her) died, only eight years before she herself passed away in 1991, was that Amy needed someone to talk to. But she was a magnificent teacher of languages, and I owe her thanks for the ones I know.

From the time I was two, we spent the northern summer months, June, July, and August, at a summer house some twenty miles from

Helsinki, in an area that was then quite rural. The surrounding culture consisted of working-class Finns with a sprinkling of vacation home owners like ourselves. Although I did not have any playmates except for my sister, and later on, for a brief period, my brother Erkki who is seven years my junior, I loved those summers and populated the landscape with long serial fantasies, stories I told myself, in which those "giant white rabbit people" were part of the cast.

nineteen thirty-nine

just sit here telling myself all these stories
when the sun is shining
on the granite & the veins in it & the veins
in the back of my father's hand
pine needles moss & the light the light
a great roaring silence
so spacious & hospitable
to the rising voice of my mind (7)

"[T]he light the light," indeed; summer days were long, but in the winter they were short and *dark*. It was dark when I set out for school in the mornings, and the streetlights were coming on again when I trudged home. And, yes, "the veins / in the back of my father's hand"—he was almost fifty years old when I was born. Compared to my mother, he *was* taciturn, but we did have long philosophical conversations and played many games of checkers during those summers; made our own bows and arrows, threw darts, wandered around the woods looking for mushrooms as Fall approached.

Poem Beginning with a Line by Edward Thomas

the steam hissed.   someone cleared his throat.
it was my father: time to get off train.
summer time
            for inward world —
rocks. plants. birds. reptiles.   mammals

other than ourselves
perceived
        in mute surmise.   three months
times ten. a great blank shining space
in life, each year,
quite probably only
        reason i'm still here. (8)

In 1944, after Finland had made a separate peace with the Soviet Union, I spent a summer on the west coast of Sweden with friends of my parents. My host family's paterfamilias had saved his favorite juvenilia, which included the collected works of James Fenimore Cooper and Edward S. Ellis, a big batch of *Buffalo Bill* and *Texas Jack* pulp novels, and Edgar Rice Burroughs' *Tarzan* saga. All in Swedish, of course. Like any Germanophone for generations, I had read Karl May's interminable novels set in an entirely imaginary Far West of the nineteenth century, but I had also read Eirik Hornborg's pioneering history of the North American "Indian wars" and was able to enjoy the various subtexts and biases all those authors presented. I was a Western nerd, the way my friend David Ball, the poet, French literature scholar, and distinguished translator of Henri Michaux (whom I was to meet six or seven years later at an international summer camp in upstate New York) was (then) a Science Fiction nerd.

Such esoteric knowledge did nothing to further my schoolwork, but my command of German, Swedish, English, and French (which Amy taught me between the ages of eight and ten) certainly did, and since I also had an aptitude for writing in the language of instruction, Finnish, and did quite well in math and science, I floated through high school at the head of my class. While I had friends among my brainier classmates, I found them dull, by and large, and admired the kids who came from less pretentious families, even submitting to a degree of bullying and condescension from these streetwise types. Everything my parents enthused about—J.A. from a humanistic-Platonic viewpoint, Amy from a Nietzschean 'will to change' vantage—that smacked of heroics, idealism, reverence for some abstruse 'virtue' or another, was deeply suspect to me. I was a politely rebellious son and student affecting the style of my not always so polite fellow rebels—1930's gangster style hats, pegged "jitterbug" pants, and a generally snotty and cool attitude to cover up typical adolescent innocence and romanticism.

Teen Angel

streets
he walked
thinking to meet or
merely to see her

once a day   or once
every other
third or
fourth

a madness

buildings   pavements
lines drawn so fine

sweet madness of centuries

there she was   no one else
only i & she

a strange
an isolate
sensibility

eternity
was

my address
then (9)

Her name was Nina, and she was Russian, although born in Helsinki. Her family had come from St. Petersburg but not from the "circles" my mother felt *we* belonged to. Amy was violently opposed to our teen-age romance—which, in a pre-automobile culture, was limited to long walks and smooching in stairwells. When, in my senior year in high school, I was encouraged by my teachers to apply for an American Field Service International scholarship to the U.S., my parents strongly seconded this, feeling it would be a Very Good Thing to put the North Atlantic and a few thousand square miles of continent between Nina and me. So, off I went—first to the aforementioned summer camp, where I met David and argued with him about the respective merits of Westerns and Science Fiction, and then to McKinley High in Cedar Rapids, Iowa.

Chingachgook and Cody, Winnetou, Wild Bill and their cohorts had been my guides across the huge, wild, entirely imaginary land across the ocean, and by my late teens, those thrilling chieftains had been joined and overshadowed by Ishmael, Huck Finn, Nick Adams, Sam Spade, Philip Marlowe, Holden Caulfield; but by the time *he* came along, I was already having a not-so-thrilling sojourn in Midwestern suburbia.

This was 1951. My hosts considered W. Somerset Maugham unsuitable reading for a seventeen-year-old, and they turned an unhealthy color when I told them I really liked Henry *The Air-Conditioned Nightmare* Miller. They certainly hadn't heard of bebop, and even if they had, they would have disapproved of it, as they disapproved of the teenagers from "downtown" Cedar Rapids with whom I struck up friendships across class lines.

Having thus acquired firsthand experience of the chasms that yawned between at least three distinct and separate "cultures" in "America" (then as now), i.e. Artistic, Official, and Popular, the kid from Helsinki, Finland returned from his first venture to the West a sadder but marginally wiser person, and left Helsinki soon thereafter for prolonged sojourns in Germany, Austria, and England, not to return to these still so curiously Divided States until 1965.

2

The first poetry I read, in a parental home with a sizable polyglot library, consisted of works by the German Romantics printed in Gothic type faces—for instance, Johann Wolfgang von Goethe's *Wer reitet so spät durch Nacht und Wind*:

> Who's riding so late through night-wind wild?
> It is the father with his child;
> He holds his boy safe from the storm,
> His cradling arm is keeping him warm.

Spine-tingling stuff, especially when we get to the Elf-King's seductive promises to the little boy:

> Do come with me, my lad so fair!
> My lovely daughters shall give thee care,
> Through night my daughters' revels sweep,
> They'll dance and they'll sing and they'll rock thee to sleep. (10)

In the end, the Elf-King steals the boy's soul; so, don't even dream of going out "riding so late through night-wind wild" (a sentiment of which my mother certainly approved). Then there was verse of a more historico-heroic orientation, such as Count August von Platen's *The Grave in the Busento*:

> Nights one hears on the Busento near Cosenza muffled singing:
> Echoes answer from the waters, from the depths seem to be
> > ringing,
> Shades of valiant Goths move back and forth in ghostly
> > lamentation,
> Mourning the death of Alaric, the greatest leader of their nation.
> > (11)

In school, there was more of that sort of thing in Finnish, easily recognizable as, indeed, more of the same. It was interspersed with readings from *The Kalevala*, the collection of Eastern Finnish oral poetry Elias Lönnrot cobbled into a "national epic" in the early nineteenth century:

> I am driven by my longing,
> And my understanding urges
> That I should commence my singing,
> And begin my recitation.
> I will sing the people's legends,
> And the ballads of the nation.
> To my mouth the words are flowing,
> And the words are gently falling,
> Quickly as my tongue can shape them,
> And between my teeth emerging. . .(12)

To a person raised both above and down below in World War II air raid shelters, in a family divided by Axis vs. Allied sympathies, glorifications of heroism and nationalist mythology were not only boring but repugnant. Long before the "Sixties," I was a confirmed internationalist, anti-militarist (though not necessarily 100% pacifist), anti-authoritarianist, anti- "Prussian." To this day, military uniforms with or without people inside them give me the heebie-jeebies. I love the "America" of early Anarchist communes, of the IWW, of the Lincoln Brigade, of the WPA, and thus feel close to the strains of the sixties that derive from that tradition.

Excursus: The Kalevala

For a Finn of my Helsinki generation, the *Kalevala* was an early obligatory task of reading and memorization. Hence, first encounters with that work were nonproductive of anything but the traditional school-boy jokes about birch-bark shoes, etc. The way schools presented the material was off-putting: It was *hyped*, much as I imagine the *Nibelungenlied* was in contemporary thirties' and forties' Germany, as the greatest literary achievement of mankind, the ancients' blessed gift to us feeble descendants. While not the product (at least, as we have it) of a Homeric intelligence, *The Kalevala* does have its charms, spells, and spell-binding moments. It deals with The Word and its Power; it contains the Osiris myth, complete, in two versions, as well as the Quest motif, and, as Paavo Haavikko, the grand old man of Finnish poetry, has demonstrated in two brilliant versions, the story of the origin of abstract "wealth." Then there are Lemminkäinen's amorous and martial exploits whose telling seems closer to the Norse sagas' world than to the ancient shamanistic ambience of blacksmith Ilmari and singer-sorcerer Väinö.

Later, it struck me how bleakly secularized the Icelandic sagas were compared to the *Kalevala* and *Kalevipoeg*, the Estonian variant of the same material. Not until my reading, at least a decade later, of traditional Native American matter did I realize that this was no accident, but due to the stubborn preservation of old traditions in certain cultures, possibly and particularly in those the nineteenth century was fond of calling backward or primitive. Then I came across Giorgio di Santillana's remarkable *Hamlet's Mill*, which resulted in a mildly embarrassing contretemps with a Finnish ambassador to the U.S. During the ten minutes preceding my modest speculative reading of Santillana's thoughts on the "Sampo" theme, at a major American city's Kalevala Day, the ambassador delivered himself of a speech to the effect that the *Kalevala* was simply so great that it did not, and should not ever, require any form of interpretation. Like Yahweh's tablets, it had to be taken at face value. . . . At the risk of sounding immodest, I would like to have it on record that I managed to retain my lunch, deliver the lecture, and walk away with a glowing new-found affection for Louhi, Kauko, Kullervo, and all those folks.

While the *Kalevala* is a typically *patriarchal* cycle of narrative poems, it reads like a revisionist document, one of the earliest: Louhi, the powerful and from our heroes' point of view vicious Lady of the Northland, is Kali, the Great Mother, capable of devouring feeble male ambassadors. Her powerful and decisive presence in the epic as we now have it may hark back to a time when battle was joined between an old shamanistic and matriarchal culture on one hand, and upstart bands of 'heroes' on the other.

Unless you *like* Longfellow's *Hiawatha*, the only readable English version of the *Kalevala* is Francis Peabody Magoun's.

There was one poet in my early reading of German classics whose words seemed to bear some relation to how I felt about things:

> The sexton's daughter was small and sweet,
> She showed me through hall and crypt;
> Her hair was blond, her form petite,
> From her neck the kerchief had slipped.
>
> Candles and crosses, tomb and fount —
> She gave me a tour of the place.
> The temperature then began to mount —
> I looked in Elsbeth's face.
> [. . .]
> The sexton's daughter sweetly led
> The way out of hall and crypt;
> Her lips were moist, her neck was red,
> From her bosom the kerchief had slipped. (13)

Like his soul brother Robert Burns, Heinrich Heine loses quite a bit in translation, but there was an irreverent Enlightenment edge to his verse that was very appealing, as were his revolutionary and cynical sentiments:

> There are two kinds of rat:
> One hungry, and one fat.
> The fat ones stay content at home,
> But hungry ones go out and roam.
> [. . .]
> These wild and savage rats
> Fear neither hell nor cats,
> They have no property, or money too,
> So they want to divide the world anew.
> [. . .]
> The burghers spring to arms,
> The priests ring out alarms.

The bulwark of the state, you see,
Is periled—namely, Property.
[. . .]
No finespun talk can help, no trick
Of old out-dated rhetoric.
Rats are not caught with fancy isms—
They leap right over syllogisms. (14)

Years later, I recognized that tone and vision again in the works of Bertolt Brecht.

"Old out-dated rhetoric" was, indeed, what I mostly found in my early reading of what was called *poetry*, even though there were exceptions such as Heine, Christian Morgenstern, the German counterpart of Lewis Carroll, and Joachim Ringelnatz, a Hamburg sailor poet who still awaits translation (and may have to wait a long time—his verse is 1920's macho-piratical and far from politically correct). e.e. cummings, Carl Sandburg, and Don Marquis were, if memory serves, discoveries made in Cedar Rapids, or even before that, in the United States Information Service library in Helsinki. Their various rhetorics struck me as more up to date.

3

To get back to my first sojourn on American soil: For reasons still not entirely clear to me, I was expelled from the dubious Eden that was Cedar Rapids. I was seventeen, and my only vices at the time were smoking cigarettes in public and masturbating in private (Diogenes would have liked it better the other way around). The AFS people were unable to relocate me anywhere, they even had trouble booking passage for me back to Finland, and so I stayed in their clubhouse in New York City for a couple of months at the beginning of 1952. Provided with a small allowance, I was free to roam the streets, museums, and bookstores. Finally, after I was shipped home, I earned my baccalaureate and matriculated at the University of Helsinki, with the intent of majoring in science, to follow in my maternal grandfather's, Paul Walden's foot-steps as a chemist—thus fulfilling my mother's "dearest wish". . . .

After a stint as an interpreter at the 1952 Olympic Games in Helsinki. and a couple of rather dismal semesters at the university (I was still pining for Nina, but she wouldn't have me back), I came down with a touch of tuberculosis and had my one and only *Magic Mountain* experience, a long summer in a sanatorium in the Finnish countryside. It has been a while since I last read Mann's novel, but it seems to me that there was a whole lot more boozing and sexual activity going on in good old Nummela. It was where I first acquired a taste for alcohol, and it was where I had my first consummated affair, with a kind and passionate older woman. I had just published my first slim volume of poems, the only ones I ever wrote in Finnish (mostly not very good imitations of Heine and Lorca, although a couple of them still lead a ghostly existence in Finnish anthologies), I had a mistress, I had nights of love and laughter with her, interspersed with nights of serious drink-ing in the company of a bunch of engagingly monstrous Ur-Finnish war veterans. I had escaped from long dreary hours in concrete-floored chemistry labs. Antibiotics and a drug called PAS had taken the sting out of the White Death, the food was good, people had new Dizzy Gillespie records—I had never felt better in my whole life.

Meanwhile, back in Helsinki, my aging father was tapping away on his old Remington Noiseless typewriter, translating the umpteenth *Horatio Hornblower* novel in order to pay for it all, a bottle of White Horse Scotch on the corner of his desk. He said he liked the label be-cause it had a lot of *text* on it.

With my mother, I had visited my grandparents in 1950 in the small South German town where they had landed after a strenuous wartime odyssey from Rostock, where incendiary bombs had destroyed their home, to Berlin, to Frankfurt, and finally to the "Kurheim Zollernalb," a combination health resort and retirement home staffed by Franciscan (Sisters of St. Clare) nuns. Although my grandmother, Wanda von Lutzau (1878-1950), was fifteen years younger than her husband Paul Walden, the strains of their life in wartime had taken a greater toll on her, and she died during that visit. After that, both my mother and my sister Irina spent time living with my grandfather and helping him with his scholarly work on the history of science. In his eighties, he still lectured on the subject at the University of Tübingen.

After I was discharged from the sanatorium in the Fall of 1953, it was decided that I should spend a period of convalescence with my grandfather and take on the (none too onerous) duties of his private secretary. I did, in fact, stay with him until his death at the age of ninety-three, in 1957.

THE WALDEN VARIATIONS (*for Robert Creeley*)

white hair
fine fringes
under the brim

old sunshine on twigs

grandpa
a sturdy
alchemist

old sunshine on twigs

*

old sunshine on twigs

& on the pigs
we ate
together
he & i

deaf alchemist
loud grandson

*

ate together

teeth fell out

& died

old sun (15)

Written twenty years later, the laconic lines commemorate four extraordinary years in the company of an extraordinary human being. A research chemist whose discovery of the "Walden inversion" still merits an entry in textbooks of organic chemistry, and a widely published writer on the history of science, my grandfather had survived two revolutions and five major wars, the loss not only of his native land but of an entire *culture* that those wars and revolutions effectively wiped out, and the loss of a beloved wife and companion of fifty years when he was eighty-seven. He had come through it all with an unshaken conviction in the future possibilities of the species, even though he was fond of quoting the German proverb "Gegen die Dummheit ist kein Kraut gewachsen" (roughly, "there's no herb that'll cure stupidity"). The twigs and the sun in the poem derive from the walks we used to take in the old landscape of the Suebian piedmont, walks punctuated by occasional rest stops on benches or old field stone walls and enlivened by stertorous conversations—he was going deaf, and I had to speak very *loudly* and *clearly* into his left ear; the pigs are a reference to the local diet in which pork chops and sausages figured quite prominently.

SPACE BALTIC

Far, far
          in the future I see

an ancient gringo baron

showing his little grand-nephew
some dusty glass-case memorabilia

in the more than half-ruined manor:

". . .yesh. . . yesh. . . we used to call that a *foot-*
ball. . ." (16)

This, the title poem of a selection of my "science fiction" poems published some years ago, retains a little of the flavor of those days. Paul
Walden was no "ancient gringo baron," but he was as much a product
of a long-lost culture as the character in the poem, and his conversation
gave me a feeling for many places and events that seemed as distant in
time as I hope the symbol of present-day U.S.American gladiator ma-
nia will seem "Far, far in the future. . . ." We did not literally inhabit a
"more than half-ruined manor" but a spacious third-floor apartment
with a panoramic view of the surrounding countryside; we did have
neighbors and acquaintances whose cottages or mansions in what was
now either East Germany or Poland had vanished in the conflagration
of World War II, and in the downstairs tavern I met and drank with
returnees from prisons and concentration camps in Siberia who had
been sent to the *Kurheim* to decompress and recover.

Having lost his parents at an early age, and being the youngest of
six children, my grandfather had been raised by his brothers, at least
two of whom were officers in the Czar's army. In the Imperial Russia of
his youth and early manhood, subjects with academic accomplishments
were given the option to substitute a (considerably longer) period of
government-related teaching work for military service, and Paul Walden,
a lifelong pacifist, made that choice. His involvement with the sciences,
and his knowledge of languages and literature, must have given him a
perspective on the world that was critical of simplistic notions of pa-
triotism.

If history is understood as 'tales of the tribe' that provide reasons
for endless revenge—as they seem to be doing to this day, even in supposedly civilized European countries—perhaps only those who are truly

'mixed' and 'exiled' can step outside of that vicious circle. I am a descendant of at least five pairs of arch-enemies of one period or another: Finn/Swede, Finn/Russian, German/Pole, Pole/Russian, Russian/German—etc., etc.; only the gods know how it multiplies back and back. . .
Excursus: The Warriors

> Colonel Walden at Pulkovo   lauded by Lenin
> in John Reed's *Ten Days that Shook the World*
>
> heard on tape on the way to Taos
> "HEY THAT'S MY GRAND-UNCLE" (17)

A few years ago, as my wife Jane and I were driving from Salt Lake City to Taos, New Mexico, we were listening to an unabridged recording of John Reed's book. This was the passage that caused my exclamation:

> The Pulkovo detachment by its valorous blow has strengthened the cause of the Workers' and Peasants' Revolution. [. . .] Revolutionary Russia and the Soviet Power can be proud of their Pulkovo detachment, acting under the command of *Colonel Walden*. Eternal memory to those who fell! etc.
> *(Italics added, as in quotes to follow)* (18)

It is a quote from a telegram sent by Leon Trotsky (not Lenin—I must have been carried away by alliteration), People's Commissar, on the thirteenth of November, 1917, two days after the engagement. Historian William Henry Chamberlin elaborates:

> Trotzky [sic] is inclined to attribute much of the credit for the successful stand of the Red troops at Pulkovo to *Colonel Walden, an old colonel who had often been wounded in battle*, who assumed command and directed the flanking operations. "It couldn't have been that he sympathized with us," writes Trotzky, "because he understood nothing. But apparently he hated Kerensky so strongly that this inspired him with temporary sympathy for us." (19)

And Isaac Deutscher, in his biography of Trotsky, sheds further light on the matter:

At this stage already Trotsky had to look round for experienced and skilled commanders. On the day after the insurrection, he and Lenin turned for help to the regular officers, hitherto the target of Bolshevik attacks. But the officers who were persuaded to appear at the Smolny cautiously refused co-operation. *Only a few desperados and careerists were ready to serve under the "illegitimate" government.* One of these, Colonel Muraviev, was chosen to command in the battle on the Pulkovo Heights; and subsequently he played a conspicuous part in the first phase of the civil war. A braggart, posing as a Left Social Revolutionary, he seems to have been moved less by sympathy with the Bolsheviks than by a grudge against Kerensky. Trotsky first received him with suspicion. But the Colonel was mettlesome, resourceful, and eager to win a prize in a seemingly hopeless assignment; and so Trotsky was captivated by his initiative and courage. *Colonel Valden* [sic], *another officer of this small group, commanded the artillery, which decided the outcome of the Pulkovo battle in favor of the Bolsheviks.* (20)

An aged, battle-scarred colonel of the Russian Imperial Army, none too swift in Trotsky's opinion, a member of a small band of "desperados and careerists" in Deutscher's, yet a survivor of many engagements and clearly a competent artillery commander—the older brother of my dear scientist grandfather Paul who wouldn't hurt a fly! And truly an agent of the Fates, on that chilly day on the Pulkovo Heights.

The old colonel's sister-in-law (I doubt that they ever met), my grandmother Wanda von Lutzau, was a descendant of another warrior: Baron Adolf von Lützow (1782-1834), a Prussian cavalry officer who commanded a legendary volunteer corps, the Black Rifles, in the War of Liberation against Napoleon Bonaparte in 1813-14. These volunteers were recruited democratically, without regard to class, education, wealth, or even nationality. Not long before one of them, the Austrian poet Theodor Körner, was killed in battle, he popularized their guerrilla exploits in a ballad, *Lützows wilde verwegene Jagd* ("Lützow's wild and daring hunt"), set to music by Carl Maria von Weber and still sung at German student gatherings. Operating mostly behind enemy lines, the Black Rifles inflicted considerable damage on the French Emperor's troops and disbanded only after his abdication. Their colors, black, red, and gold, are now the colors of the German flag.

I never met my Uncle Väinö, my father's younger brother, because he sacrificed his life to the cause of the White Guard in the early stages of Finland's Civil War in 1918. A promising young architect, he was running a consignment of machine guns for his (ultimately victorious) side in the conflict, transporting them single-handedly in a horse-drawn sleigh, when he was overtaken and killed by a detachment of Red Guards. My father did not speak of him often, but when he did, I sensed his grief and regret over not having been able to curb Väinö's urge to become a martyr.

It may seem strange that I, a self-professed pacifist who was glad to be saved from military service by the dread specter of "consumption," am erecting this small verbal cenotaph for three warrior kinsmen. I think my main motivation is a sense of marvel, mixed with dismay, over the "causes" and allegiances for which males of the species are willing to sacrifice their own and others' lives. *Dulce et decorum est / pro patria mori* ("Sweet and fitting it is / to die for your fatherland"): that line of Roman state propaganda was engraved in gold letters on a marble slab in my Finnish high school's assembly hall, and I remember shuddering at its coercive hypocrisy every time I noticed it.

4

stand up a berserker   end up a beseecher
in the vast stone forest of the world's war memorials

the ghosts of generals stumble about
disheveled confused   graffiti on the great moving wall

moving toward The Wall   résumés for god
Papa wanted me to marry the Finnish language

Mama   chemistry .   (her father's life)
both kept me away from Finnish-speaking women
        with all their might

so I went to Germania & married a German speaker
but couldn't make a living in those countries

so ended up in England   thus changing
my great love affair with the English (specifically
        American)

language into a lifetime commitment/marriage (21)

All true. No poetic license there. I met Josephine Clare Wirkus, an
aspiring actress, in her Suebian home town Gammertingen where I
spent my years with Paul Walden. After he died at his desk, fountain
pen skittering away from an unfinished sentence, I returned to Helsinki
for a brief time at my parents' home. During my years with him I had
kept on writing literary reviews and essays for Finnish newspapers and
magazines, while also pursuing a brief 'career' as a writer in German
that resulted in a handful of published short stories and poems. (22)
Not unreasonably, my parents felt that there was no 'future' in this, and
they urged me to go back to the university to get a degree, and to forget
my truelove in Germany who, while an improvement on former Russian and Finnish girlfriends, still was not what they had in mind for me.
    She was what I had in mind, though, and after working a few months
as a translator/secretary for a lumber firm and saving my pennies, I
took off for Vienna, where Josephine was finishing her acting studies
with a professor of the Max Reinhardt school, and simply arrived on
her doorstep one late summer evening. . .

EXCITING MOMENTS OF THE PAST #631

sit in shrub
wait for errant lover

thinking of politics
in 1956 (23)

We moved in together, got married in the winter, and eked out a strenuous existence in the—for us, somewhat ironically named—Wohllebengasse ("Street of Good Living"). Josephine worked evenings as a waitress, I had a stint as a menial worker for the Atomic Energy Agency and another in the employ of the Vienna Trade Fair; I still wrote the occasional piece for publication in Finland (an essay on the great Austrian novelist Heimito von Doderer, an interview with Thornton Wilder when he visited the city), Josephine continued her studies, and we held tight and got by. Vienna in the late fifties was not the worst place to be young, and in love, and two against the world.

Excursus: Poetry

It wasn't until I encountered the monumentally baffling Ezra Pound—at first, I believe, in a bilingual edition with Eva Hesse's (24) remarkable German translations: a small paperback selection with a greenish photo image of the slightly puffy-faced poet on a glossy black cover—that poetry began to seem a subject worthy of active pursuit. Pound's Bertran de Born still smacked of mothball heroics, but *Cathay* and *The Cantos* were something else. They existed in a realm of active language first opened up to me by Ernest Hemingway's crisply Imagist short stories, the favorite reading matter of my early twenties. They also led me to the work of William Carlos Williams and helped me identify my dissatisfaction with my own attempts to write Heinesque poems and Hemingwayesque short stories. WCW's poems encompassed more of what human life was about most of the time, and did so with greater economy, elegance, and variousness than those ultimately formulaic 'stories':

Somebody dies every four minutes
in New York State ——

To hell with you and your poetry ——
You will rot and be blown

through the next solar system
with the rest of the gases ——

What the hell do you know about it ?

AXIOMS

Don't get killed. . . (26)

Compared to the poems of Williams and Pound even the prose of
Chekhov and Stendhal *ran on rails*, just as what poetry I knew from the
nineteenth and most previous centuries seemed to do: this new poetry
made it possible to get off the train and fly through galaxies and dande-
lions, zoom down to a nail in a woman's shoe, up to the top of Niagara
Falls, back to a sunset over Mount Taishan or forward to some minus-
cule personal moment of incredible complexity in an undisclosed, wholly
interior location. Williams', Louis Zukofsky's, and Kenneth Rexroth's
essays mapped the European sources of that kind of vision—Apollinaire,
Cendrars, Reverdy, and Garcia Lorca; the last-mentioned I had already
discovered through an intermediary, one "Georges Forestier" who, in
the 1950s, sold thousands of copies of his book *Ich schreibe mein Herz in
den Staub der Strasse* ("I Inscribe My Heart in the Dust of the Road") by
presenting it as the work of a Byronic Alsatian-born Foreign Legion-
naire. The poems were blatant imitations of Lorca, and "Forestier" was
soon revealed as a fiction (or fraud, depending on how judgmental you
want to be); nevertheless, I am still grateful to him for pointing my way
to one of the masters.

Despite the ruins and losses and pervasive feelings of guilt and resentment, the fifties in central and northern Europe were an exhilarating time. Artists and poets of post-World War II "free" Europe were
rediscovering and catching up on the spectacular modernist movements
that had emerged and flourished between the wars: Cubism, Futurism,

Dada, Surrealism, Joyce, Pound, Kafka, Stein—all that had been either banned or buried for almost a decade, especially (with the exception of Switzerland) in the Germanophone realm.

During my years in Germany and Austria, I attended that revival both as a reader and, to a modest extent, as a writer. German poet-editors Kurt Leonhard, Max Bense, and Reinhard Döhl were kind enough to publish and even anthologize some of my German-language texts—these were now influenced by Dada, Bense's "stochastic" experiments (27) based on probability theory and cybernetics, and Helmut Heissenbüttel's post-Steinian writings. (In parenthesis: in the mid-to-late sixties I encountered a very similar "language orientation" in work produced by students of mine, mavericks at the Iowa Writers' Workshop—whom I introduced to the relatively few translations that were then available of that German-language oeuvre, including works by h.c. artmann and Konrad Bayer of the Vienna Group of the Fifties (28) and to some of these writers' major initial influences—Sapir, Whorf, Wittgenstein, Barthes, and others.)

Collage and montage of various kinds were the major modes of production. "Any text could be used, textbooks, trivial literature, etc., and [. . .] the effect is that of releasing language from its rules and structure, demonstrating its restrictions and hierarchies. The idea that language molds and shapes thought is not new, dating from at least the 19th century, but the Vienna Group made this their basic literary premise." (29)

In a note I wrote for my section in a German anthology published in 1963, I see an early expression of my continued love-hate relationship with that "artful" approach to poetry: "I've experimented with various techniques of fractured syntax, mostly in German, but find that the results end up being merely the charmingly sinister effects of a kind of insensate 'objectivity,' a dead end. Time to start over, however modestly." (30)

Little did I know, then, that it is *always* time to start over. However modestly.

5

Late in 1957, I received in the mail an advertisement from a Helsinki newspaper. The British Broadcasting Corporation's European Services, whose brief was "Projection of Britain," were looking for a Programme Assistant for their Finnish Section, to work on short-wave radio broadcasts from London to Finland. At one of Josephine's tables in the outdoor wine garden of Hübner's Kursalon in the City Park of Vienna, I penned a handwritten application much in the same spirit in which I now fill out sweepstake forms, not expecting anything to come of it.

I did, however, receive a reply. Martin Esslin, who was then working for the BBC's European Services and would later rise to prominence as Head of BBC Drama in both radio and television, and who is the author of pioneering books on the life of Bertolt Brecht and the Theatre of the Absurd, was coming to Vienna on Corporation business and would be glad to interview me for the job. Our meeting went well, I was hired, and from the beginning of 1958 to mid-1967 Josephine and I lived in London.

Those nine years in the United Kingdom mostly confirmed the premonition I had when we left Vienna—that London was a place where I would find few writers with an urgency to "start over" in any direction not sanctioned by the established consensus of a venerable tradition. Dada and Surrealism, in their day, had made no perceptible dents in that consensus; they had just been aberrant "Continental" fads. There never had been an Armory Show in London, yet it was mainly among visual artists (Richard Hamilton, R.B. Kitaj, Ian Hamilton Finlay, Edoardo Paolozzi, Alan Davie, Tom Phillips) that one found a lively sense of what had been thought and done elsewhere in the first half of the century. The Brits were kind, and I made life-long friends there, but the literary power structure was afflicted by a closed shop mentality. Pound had come and gone; Eliot was a gray eminence glimpsed slouching toward the elevator in Bush House, the headquarters of the BBC's European and Overseas Services; and Basil Bunting had not yet been resurrected— a few people knew and appreciated his work and that of David Jones and David Gascoyne, but they were not among the taste-makers of the period of "Angry Young Men" playwrights and "Movement" poets.

As Allen Ginsberg remarked when we first met in London, the young Britons who worshiped the Stones and the Beatles were not *readers*: The early "Beat" era produced no British counterparts to Kerouac, Ginsberg, Corso, and Ferlinghetti across the Atlantic. There were imitators, but a genuine assimilation of the Beat, Black Mountain, and New York School aesthetic only took place in the late Sixties and early Seventies, largely due to the influence of American poets Edward Dorn, Tom Clark, and Ted Berrigan who spent time teaching, editing, and publishing in the UK. In retrospect, Allen's observation may have reflected the economic and educational difference between U.S. and U.K. collegiate cultures in the Sixties.

I still have a vivid personal memory of my excitement and delight upon finding *Howl* and *Gasoline* in a book shop in the Charing Cross Road, and soon I acquired friends and mentors among those who felt a similar delight: Michael Shayer and Gael Turnbull who published *Migrant* magazine and my first book in English, (31) Tom Raworth (who published *Outburst* and, with Barry Hall, Goliard Press books), and Michael Horovitz (*New Departures*). We looked to the poets we read in U.S.American magazines like Cid Corman's *Origin*, LeRoi Jones' *Yugen*, Diane Di Prima's *Floating Bear*, Lita Hornick's *Kulchur*—then met them in the flesh as they came to visit and some even to stay a while in "Swinging London": Allen; Gregory Corso, who became my daughter's godfather; Lawrence Ferlinghetti, who published my translations of *Red Cats*; (32) Robert Creeley; Edward Dorn; Jerome Rothenberg; Jonathan Williams; John Ashbery; Ronald Johnson; Tom Clark; Peter Orlovsky; Aram Saroyan; Lewis MacAdams; Gerard Malanga; Larry Fagin; David Ball (first met in New York in 1951!); Piero Heliczer. . . .

Excursus: "Un marginal. . ."

One bright August day in 1993, Jane and I drive up into the mountains. Browsing in Nederland's shoppes, I find a blue stone and a copy of *The Brief Hour of François Villon* by John Erskine, author of many popular books in the thirties (including *The Private Life of Helen of Troy*, which I remember reading in the American Field Service clubhouse in New

York); good subjects, watery works. And in the mail back in Boulder, there is a card from Tom Raworth to tell me: "Piero was killed in a traffic accident in France a few days ago. Bad, so his widow says—hit by a truck." Leaving his enterprise with pain and cry. . . . His father, *un dottore*, partisan, died in World War II, fighting the Nazis in Italy. Piero Heliczer—"*un marginal*" in the French newspaper story Tom had sent me a month earlier, all about Piero's getting dragged out of bed and beaten up by pea-brained humanoids. His enterprise, "underground" movies in the heady days of Harry Smith and Jack Smith and Andy Warhol, and before that, small handset books and broadsides that were *petits grimoires*, secret scrolls, prayer flags. And, what else *are* true poems? We were friends in London, in the Sixties. His poems still await a collected edition.

Donald M. Allen's anthology *The New American Poetry 1945-1960* (32) was the answer to the prayers of our little cargo cult—evidence that there were not just one or two or three poets "over there" who had heard and assimilated the sounds of the mid-twentieth century, but at least forty-four, and, as the editor stated, this selection presented only a fraction of their work. Piero wasn't in it, though, and I remember him complaining about this, although he did admire Ebbe Borregaard's work in the book.

Excursus: Translation

My job with "Auntie," a.k.a. "The Beeb," involved a great deal of translation, and since my salary was not exactly munificent though adequate for people of frugal habits, I augmented it by free-lance translations. There were times during the London years when I felt that I had three full-time jobs: my five days a week at Bush House, translation commissions from various Finnish publishers, and my own work in English— not to mention being the father of three children. . .

Translation can make you say things you would otherwise never say in your 'own' language. As experience has shown me, even translations from a closely related historical / cultural / linguistic sphere into the translator's main, thoroughly lived-in, and actively used hist./cult./ling. sphere, can present problems of a kind I would call *auratic*, i.e., to do with the "auras" of words, lines or sentences, stanzas or paragraphs. Even the best dictionaries are just rickety little ladders to raise against the walls between those linguistic spaces. Thus, for instance, a good literary translator from Swedish into English has to deal with the fact that the Swedish lexicon (= vocabulary) is much smaller than the English one: in order not to make the English version sound like babytalk, s/he has to determine the "aura" of nouns, verbs, adjectives in their original environment, and then has to find, select, the English terms that most closely correspond to that aura in his/her text. In the case of translation from languages whose entire tradition is significantly different from one's own, these auratic problems can become huge.

The idea of translation was one I literally grew up with. As I have already mentioned, my father, J. A. Hollo, was a well-known and prolific translator of world literature into Finnish, from Cervantes to Tolstoy to Flaubert to Henry James. My mother translated scholarly Finnish texts into German, which was her first spoken language, and subsequently—well, both subsequently and *consequently*—my first spoken language as well.

As noted earlier, I learned to *read* from a Swedish ABC book, when my sister got tired of reading and translating the comic strips in Stockholm newspapers to me—and so, I learned a six-year-old person's Swedish at the same time. (My return to Sweden four years later, and the reading I did then, implanted a lasting and continued affection for that language and its literature.) Back in Helsinki, my father taught me Finnish so that I would be ready for school. Then came English, by the age of ten, by means of lessons given by my mother and later in school; French and high school Latin followed. As inhabitants of the Baltic region know—along with those of other polylingual parts of the world where speakers of different languages more or less manage to coexist— there was really nothing extraordinary about that; my sister and brother went on to become fluent in Russian, which I never managed beyond its (now long-forgotten) alphabet. *Red Cats* and other versions from the Russian were produced in collaboration with my mother and other Russian scholars.

I certainly did not, and never will, match my father's working knowledge of fourteen different languages, demonstrated in a lifetime as a literary translator. Nor have I, with my first childhood memories marked by a world war, ever been as serenely confident of the ultimate human value of Goethe's concept of "world literature," and the attendant importance of literary translation, as he must have been at least in the beginning of his career.

Nevertheless, I first read *Don Quixote*, *War and Peace*, and *Crime and Punishment* in his elegant Finnish, and during my London years I embarked on translations into Finnish on a far more modest scale. Looking back, the most memorable results of those endeavors were two little volumes of John Lennon's writings and a number of poems by Allen Ginsberg and Robert Creeley published in literary magazines and anthologies. In the early sixties, I also collaborated with Josephine on booklength German translations of Ginsberg, Gregory Corso, and the daddy of them all, William Carlos Williams. (33)

In a way, Bush House was an extension of my parental home, another miniature Tower of Babel within whose walls it seemed possible to work with several languages like a juggler, keeping two or three or four balls in the air at the same time. As the years went by, it became apparent that I could not continue that juggling act ad infinitum—that I had to commit myself to one language before the others. For most of my adult life, U.S.American English has been my waking and dreaming language.

I had left Helsinki in the early fifties for Germany, Austria, and then Britain, and outside of the offices and studios of Bush House had no active spoken use of Finnish. From my early teens, English and American English literature had been my favored reading matter, and after that slim volume of adolescent verse in Finnish, and a few poems in German, I had not attempted to write my own poetry in anything but English.

It occurred to me that some of the poetry coming out of Finland in the post-WW II era, notably the work of Paavo Haavikko, Tuomas Anhava, Eeva-Liisa Manner, and Pentti Saarikoski, shared something with the new wave of American poets: in their work, I saw a willingness to open up new forms radically different from those employed by predecessors, and a tendency to favor concreteness and vivid imagery over idealistic abstraction and breathy symbolism. These two post-war generations of poets, widely separated in terms of geography and language, shared a common discovery—one might say, rediscovery—of the rich modernist tradition of the poetry of France, Russia, Spain, and Italy in the early decades of the century.

Poets and writers of the two post-war Germanies and Austria, emerging from inquisitorial state censorship of the arts, were also rebuilding their bridges back to the twenties and early thirties. By the early sixties they found capable English and American translators—Jerome Rothenberg, Michael Hamburger, Christopher Middleton, to name but three who are significant poets in their own right. Eric Bentley had also begun his pioneering translations of Brecht. So, that field looked well-tilled, and apart from one Brecht play, *Jungle of Cities*, (34) and some poems by Paul Klee, (35) Helmut Heissenbüttel, and Günter Grass, I left it to those capable hands and concentrated on Paavo Haavikko and Pentti Saarikoski. Booklength selections of both their work appeared in London in the late sixties and became part of the heady internationalism of the poetry and music scene of those years. A quarter of a century later, I am still actively engaged with the work of Finnish poets, and those two in particular. I have expanded their Anglophone bibliographies since then. (36) With the unstinting support of Marja-Leena Rautalin of the Finnish Literature Information Center I have been able to complete translations from numerous other Finnish writers of various genres, and hope to continue doing so. Finding texts worthy of translation is no problem at all—finding *publishers*, in a world in the process of becoming more interconnected on one hand and more fractious and provincial on the other, is a tougher proposition. Thirty years as a literary translator have made me resigned to the fact that the Anglophone world is indifferent to literature from numerically small (or should I say, politically marginal?) European languages. Nobel Prizes and major political upheavals may kindle temporary interest in such works, but on the whole, apart from, say, the occasional new version of Finland's national epic, the *Kalevala*, Finnish literature in translation does not often appear in the lists of U.S. publishers.

6

Socially and anthropologically, the early sixties in London were a lively time. Thanks to my job with the BBC, and to Josephine's active interest in the theater, we were able to see great productions of the work of that period's playwrights, actors, and directors. Working for "Auntie," I interviewed a number of British writers, among them Rebecca West, L.P. Hartley, Angus Wilson, Alan Sillitoe; wrote radio dramatizations of works like Rudyard Kipling's *The Man Who Would Be King*; DJ'ed a jazz show on Sunday afternoons; reviewed plays and movies; met John Lennon and Yoko Ono at a gallery opening of Yoko's works; met the "Beats" and their British emulators, some of whom camped in the basement of our building and climbed four flights of stairs to use our bathroom. . . . There were parties, boozy Fleet Street lunches, poetry readings. . . . It was life in the Yellow Submarine, all right, but for me, it was also the time of becoming a family man: all three of our children were born in London. Looking back, I realize that Josephine and I were operating at incredible speeds, both physically and psychologically—as was, or so it seemed, just about everybody else we knew.

In the present moment's memory remake, Anselm Hollo ca. 1963 looks like an astonishing composite: good provider type, riding the double-decker bus to work five days a week—industrious translator and literary reporter—father of one, two, three young children—and poet, or at least yearning to be of that number. Many of my works from the period now strike me as curiously, almost *programmatically* out of touch— or *only* in touch with a fantasy world infused with "the new spirit" epitomized by the Beats, the New York School, the Beatles, The Incredible String Band, the whole kit and kaboodle floating above those years that also saw the Cuban missile crisis, the assassination of JFK, and (then as now) seemingly endless insensate strife on all continents.

Nevertheless, those works met with some attention. Critic A. Alvarez nicknamed me the "Beatnik Walter De La Mare," poet George MacBeth invited me to read on the Third Programme, and Edward Lucie-Smith and Martin Bax were instrumental in publishing my collections in handsome editions. Jerome Rothenberg arranged an invitation to a literary

6

conference in New York City, and Paul Blackburn introduced my first-ever reading on American soil at the then still embryonic St. Mark's Poetry Project.

All this proved a little too heady for my already scattered brains (William Carlos Williams: "I am he / whose brains are scattered / aimlessly"). I fell in love with a young woman in New York, returned to London desolate at having had to leave her to go back to family and job, and thus joined the ranks of victims of the era. The Englishman (or other European, but the "Brit" in particular) who finds himself in the New World of the academic, artistic, literary sixties (or even seventies) and succumbs to its drugs, sex, and rock and roll, plunging his hitherto humdrum existence into total if at times joyful chaos, is a staple figure in many novels of the period. I fell right into that pattern, and it followed me across the Atlantic again when I was invited to teach summer school at SUNY Buffalo, then to the Writers' Workshop in Iowa City, Iowa—only fourteen miles from Cedar Rapids, where I had been put on a midnight bus to New York back in '51. . . .

My anima-chasing, to use a Jungian term that may sound too polite but that, I believe, truly describes my compulsion, and my steadily attendant addiction to alcohol put severe strains on my marriage, but our family held together through our six years in Iowa City. I think that the death of my father in 1967 made a deeper impression on me than I was prepared to admit at the time. It probably brought up fears that I, myself, was in no way ready to be a father, and these fears in turn made me reject the role and want to insist on all my anarcho-bohemian freedoms.

> where was it i
> fell asleep in the afternoon
> & down
> & into a hall
> where forceful as ever in her big chair
> he who was i there saw her
> hum to a thin corner shadow
> the brother pale rigid
> not a sound then the sister

energy out of a door on the right
but i knew where he lay
went on & entered
the room light & bare
no curtains no books
his head on the pillow
hand moving outward
the gesture "be seated"
i started talking, saw myself from the back
leaned forward, talked to his face
intent, bushy-browed
eyes straining to see
into mine
"a question i wanted to ask you"
would never know what it was
but stood there & was
so happy to see him
that twenty-sixth day of april
three months after his death (37)

Excursus: Iowa City

I could easily wax boring about my Iowa City years, a time I still believe unequalled in that place for intellectual and artistic excitement and innovation, marked, as it was, by the presence of a succession of important and often atypical mentors at the Writers' Workshop (Ted Berrigan, Kathleen Fraser, Seymour Krim, Jack Marshall, Steve Katz, George Starbuck among them) and the equally vigorous presence of spirited young poets either getting their MFA degrees or living and working in the city, including Alice Notley, now one of the major poets of our time; Merrill Gilfillan, now known to a wide public as an important essayist on the Western Plains region; the late Darrell Gray, one of this country's first truly "postmodernist" poets, wonderfully unprogrammatic and hence regrettably unacknowledged to this day; Barrett Watten and Bob Perelman, later founders of the still active and influential

L=A=N=G=U=A=G=E school and its *Poetics Journal*; Dave Morice, inventor of *Poetry Comics*; John Sjoberg, David Hilton, George Mattingly. . . The 'foreign' poets, visitors to the International Writing Program: Gunnar Harding, Tomaz Salamun, Nicholas Born, Juan Agustin Palazuelos, Ryuichi Tamura. . .

"Those were the days, my friend. . ." After Iowa City, I became a member of what has been called "the gypsy scholars of the seventies," a generation of itinerant poet-teachers, most of whom found themselves out of jobs in the eighties—being retired early, as it were, having taught in fifteen different places in as many years. I was lucky to land a few stints that allowed me to stay longer than a year, but this peripatetic existence made it impossible for me to stay with my family, who finally were neither willing nor able to break camp every other year for yet another visiting gig of mine.

AUTOBIOGRAPHICAL BROADCASTING CORPORATION

eight years behind a microphone—blip—

then bid farewell to normal speak (39)

That farewell had been quite a relief. On the other hand, it had also been a farewell to what is known as a "stable existence."

In the main, my life has proceeded along the lines of Guy Debord's *dérive* (an ideologized form of good or bad old "drift," as in "drifter"—!), combined with a genuine love of exile, i.e., communities and places of *choice* that are not predetermined by accidents of birth. South and West have been the main directions; so, here I am now, in the American Southwest, in a town of the Front Range of the Rockies.

Greater minds have had many things to say about exile. I believe exile is (and always has been, in historical times) the basic condition of the artist. In order to see things in ways not circumscribed by conventional social perceptions, an artist has to move *outside*. That may well be the leap from traditional craft to art—the leap outside the common, outside the family, "beyond the pale." In that sense, exile may be universal. In one form or another, it is experienced by anyone who has ever woken up to what Ted Berrigan spoke of in a lecture he gave in 1982 at The Naropa Institute (in whose Jack Kerouac School of Poetics I am now happy to be teaching):

> The arts are something given to human beings to do
> They improve your senses
> It is necessary to do more than earn your daily bread
> Shelter & food & ability to get the medicine
> For your children when they have a cold
> It's necessary to be more of a person than that (40)

I was born into a family that was "in exile." I had a weird, built-in, westward drift. I didn't plan it that way. As a child, I read Westerns. Melville says "Be true to the dreams of your youth." Now I live within fifty miles of Buffalo Bill Cody's grave. Elsewhere, I have said: "*Permanent diaspora*—the ideal state."

Ted also said:

> Survival
>   is the hardest test for a poet (41)

7

Buffalo, New York; Iowa City, Iowa; Bowling Green, Ohio; Geneva, New York; Ann Arbor and East Lansing, Michigan; Baltimore, Maryland; Marshall, Minnesota; Sweet Briar, Virginia; San Francisco; Salt Lake City; Boulder, Colorado—these have been some of my way stations as a "visiting dude." Great places, all of them, but mainly in their off-campus parts (except for the libraries).

My advice to aspiring poets today would be to get a couple of Ph.D.'s before attempting a career as writers-in-residence in programs associated with academic (mostly "English") departments. Only then, if they have the right stuff, will they be able to deal with the *other* Ph.D.'s in those departments who are *not* writers, who have spent a very long stretch of their adult lives acquiring their Ph.D.'s, and who basically regard living writers with negative feelings ranging from distrust to resentment to unconcealed hatred. For them, the only good writer is a dead writer.

The sixties' dream of writing schools staffed by practicing writers of originality and wit, preferably ones who had *not* gone to writing schools, or had at least spent a decade or so doing something else for a living, has for the most part turned out to be just another sixties' dream. . . I remember thinking, back then, that the writers' workshop was the U.S.American answer to the coffeehouses and taverns of old Vienna, Paris, London—simply a *place* where writers, young, middle-aged, and old, could gather and form groups and cliques and movements and feel that they *had* a place in the world.

The United States has never had such a culture, and "creative writing programs," I argued, were at least a kind of surrogate for it. Perhaps they still are, to some extent, despite their penchant for departmental bulletin boards on which students and faculty post their latest literary scalps ("X has had a poem, 'Stars Above My Catamaran,' accepted by *The New Yorker*" "Y's story 'Gaping Genders' will appear in *The Atlantic*"), fostering yet another version of troglodytic competitiveness.

But enough of that. Despite its ups and downs, it has not been a bad life so far. Back in 1985 I managed to kick the alcohol habit, and my doors of perception have grown brighter for it. Although we are separated by great geographical distances, my children, Hannes, Kaarina, and Tamsin, and their mother Josephine and I have become a little closer in spirit again, and I feel blessed by the gods. In 1983, those gods were even kinder to me when they guided me up a very dark staircase, to Jane Dalrymple, who became my dearest friend, lover, and wife.

> though but a weave of dust and shade
> caught in the chandelle of our days
>
> who writing shovels grief's doubloons
> I can say this: hello! dear woman I name Dream

dear called *Because*
with you, a thousand years would not be long enough (42)

This autobiographical essay, however, is beginning to feel more than long enough, at least for the time being. My apologies for its hops, skips, and jumps; I realize that I have been concentrating on things I may be the only one to know—hence, on earlier years. At the moment of this writing, my three decades in this country still have many more living witnesses than do those distant European times.

Notes

(All titles, except where otherwise noted, are by the author.)

1   *Outlying Districts* (Minneapolis: Coffee House Press, 1990), p. 61.
2   Eugene Winograd and Ulrich Neisser, *Affect and Accuracy in Recall* (Cambridge: Cambridge University Press, 1993).
3   *Finite Continued* (Berkeley: Blue Wind Press, 1980), p. 21. "maternity home" in this poem follows British usage (= "maternity hospital").
4   *Heavy Jars* (West Branch, Iowa: The Toothpaste Press, 1977), p. 9.
5   *Sensation* (Buffalo: The Institute of Further Studies, 1972), p. 57.
6   *Maya* (London and New York: Cape Goliard Press and Grossman Publishers, 1970), p. 100.
7   *Sensation* (op. cit.), p. 59.
8   *No Complaints* (West Branch, Iowa: The Toothpaste Press,1983), p. 25.
9   *Finite Continued* (op. cit.), p. 45.
10 *Erlkönig* by Johann Wolfgang von Goethe. English translation (*Elf-King*) by Martin Zwart, in *A Treasury of German Ballads* (New York: Frederick Ungar, 1964), p. 50.
11 *Das Grab im Busento* by August von Platen. English translation (*The Grave in the Busento*) by Martin Zwart, in *A Treasury of. . .*(op. cit.), p. 255.
12 *Kalevala, The Land of Heroes. Verse translation by W.F. Kirby* (London and New York: John Dent and E.P. Dutton, 1907), opening lines.

13 *Im Dome* by Heinrich Heine. English translation (*In the Cathedral*) by Hal Draper, in *The Complete Poems of Heinrich Heine, A Modern English Version* (Oxford: Oxford University Press, 1982), p. 289a.

14 *Die Wanderratten* by Heinrich Heine. English translation (*The Roving Rats*) by Hal Draper, in *The Complete Poems of. . .* (op. cit.), p. 783.

15 *Black Book* (Center Conway, New Hampshire: Walker's Pond Press, 1974), pp. 38-9. Present, revised version in *Sojourner Microcosms: New and Selected Poems 1959—1977* (Berkeley: Blue Wind Press, 1977), p. 213.

16 *Space Baltic* (Mountain View, CA: Ocean View Books, 1991), p. 82.

17 From *Arcana Gardens*, in *Outlying Districts* (op. cit.), p. 107.

18 John Reed, *Ten Days that Shook the World* (London: Penguin Books, 1977), p. 199.

19 William Henry Chamberlin, *The Russian Revolution 1917—1921* (Princeton, New Jersey: Princeton University Press, 1987), p. 331.

20 Isaac Deutscher, *The Prophet Armed* (New York and London: Oxford University OPress, 1954), p. 328.

21 From *Arcana Gardens* (op. cit.), pp. 94-5

22 Some of these were collected in the anthology *Zwischenräume* ("Interstices") (Wiesbaden: Limes Verlag, 1963), pp. 26-39.

23 *Near Miss Haiku: praises laments aphorisms reports* (Chicago: Yellow Press, 1990), p. 4.

24 Not the American visual artist of the same name.

25 From *XXV* in *Spring and All* by William Carlos Williams. A. Walton Litz and Christopher McGowan, Editors: *The Collected Poems of William Carlos Williams, Volume I: 1909-1939* (New York: New Directions, 1986), pp. 231-2.

26 *augenblick* ("moment"), a literary review published and edited by Max Bense from Siegen, Germany, 1955-1961. Also: Max Bense, *Programmierung des Schönen* ("Programming the Beautiful") (Baden-Baden: Agis-Verlag, 1962).

27 See Rosmarie Waldrop and Harriett Watts, Translator-Editors, *The Vienna Group: 6 Major Austrian Poets* (Station Hill, New York: Station Hill Press, 1985).

28 Malcolm Green, Editor and translator, *Selected Works of Konrad Bayer* (London: Atlas Press, 1986), p. 7.

29 *Zwischenräume* (op. cit.), p. 26.

30   *& It Is a Song* (Birmingham: Migrant Press, 1965).

31   *Red Cats: Poems by Yevgeni Yevtushenko, Semyon Kirsanov, Andrei Voznesensky. English Versions by Anselm Hollo* (SanFrancisco: City Lights Books, 1962). See also *Red Cats Revisited,* in AHOE (Erie CO: Smoke-proof Press, 1997).

32   Donald M. Allen, Editor, *The New American Poetry 1945-1960* (New York: Grove Press, 1960).

33   William Carlos Williams, *Paterson. Deutsch von Anselm und Josephine Hollo* (Stuttgart: Henry Goverts Verlag, 1970).

34   Bertolt Brecht, *Jungle of Cities and Other Plays* (New York: Grove Press, 1965).

35   Paul Klee, *Some Poems by Paul Klee. Translated by Anselm Hollo* (Lowestoft, Suffolk: Scorpion Press, 1962).

36   Paavo Haavikko, *Selected Poems. Translated from the Finnish by Anselm Hollo* (Manchester: Carcanet Press, 1991.) Pentti Saarikoski, *Poems 1958-1980. Translated from the Finnish by Anselm Hollo* (West Branch, Iowa: Toothpaste Press, 1983). Pentti Saarikoski, *Trilogy. Translated by Anselm Hollo* (Los Angeles: Sun & Moon, 1999).

37   *Sensation* (op. cit.), p. 61.

38   *Sojourner Microcosms* (op. cit.), p. 156

39   Anselm Hollo, *Lines From Ted: An Ars Poetica.* Sonnet VI. In *Corvus* (Minneapolis: Coffee House Press, 1995).

40   Stephen Kuusisto, Deborah Tall, and Daniel Weiss, Editors, *Taking Note: From Poets' Notebooks* (Geneva, New York: Seneca Review Press, 1991), p. 82.

41   *Lines From Ted. . .* (op. cit.).

42   *West Is Left on the Map* (Boulder, Colorado: Dead Metaphor Press, 1993), last page.

Talk

AH: I LOVE THE WAY this is in our program as, simply, "Talk." I thought of titles for it. And one I thought of, totally facetiously, was "Writing Builds Character"—which is obviously untrue. A variation on that, maybe a little more true—truer—would be "Writing Builds Characters," and certainly fiction writing does that, and some poetry does that too. But the truest of all would be "Writing *Uses* Characters," and that, of course, goes two ways too: using characters whom you know, but also using the characters of writing, i.e., letters.

But that's not really what this lecture is about. Nor is it about the Inner Sibling or anything like that. It's about—basically it's about theft—stealing, borrowing, appropriation in its, I would say, apolitical and universal sense. I don't know if there's any difference between the political and the universal—but when we talk of appropriation these days we often think about, well, you know, Elvis Presley, where did he get it?, and so forth. But simply about using material that is already there, that exists in writing, possibly even on tape, record, you know—any kind of record. And doing things with it and to it. This obviously has a long history in the arts in general.

Poets have certainly always borrowed from one another. We all stand on the shoulders of giants. (1) We all occasionally like to deck ourselves out with other birds' feathers—D.H. Lawrence used that metaphor; he disapproved very strongly. But in the visual arts I think it's been a particularly clear twentieth century aesthetic phenomenon. And there are various levels to this. There's obviously the *found* piece of writing—the found poem, or found story. All stories are "found," essentially. And of course *trobar*—as in troubadour—*trobar,* the verb, to be a poet, means to *find* things. *Invent* and *find* are very close. But in the visual arts I'm sure most of you know about Marcel Duchamp's famous urinal, and his famous bicycle wheel, and his famous bottle rack. All of them, found objects that are sculptures. Yeah, this microphone is a sculpture. If you can think of a good title for it, it's yours, you know. So that's one level. But that's not to say that there aren't good found poems, but it's somewhat limited, and a little boring, mostly, or they're one-shot deals. I mean, you say, "Ha-ha, well, that was a remarkable story wasn't it? Why not?"

What happens, though—I mean, then the other part of that, which enters both into the found and shall we call it the *treated* work, is *framing*. It depends on the frame you put it in. The fashionable lit-crit word for that is—like, we don't say "theft," we say "appropriation." We don't say "framing," we say "contextualization." So, in other words, you find something that has an "original" intent, and you look at it, and you realize that by giving it another title it might read very differently.

Let's see, framing. Well, framing enters into the treated work as well; I have a note here to remember to mention Duchamp's "Mona Lisa," which is a reproduction of da Vinci's "Mona Lisa," but Duchamp added a little mustache and a little goatee to it, and at the time I suppose it still had an element of sacrilege, which it now no longer does. I mean it's just a graffito. And he has a great very funny title for it (2) which I urge you to look up, but basically what it says is "Well, you know, we can't do better than this, can we? So what can we do? The only thing left for us to do is this totally childish thing." You know?

Now I think I'll start out with my main example, my "own" example of what I'm talking about here, which is this work called "Lines from Ted: An Ars Poetica." I guess there's no pun intended in the "Ars"—it's just Latin and poetics. I guess you don't really have to say that in U.S.America, do you? But since we have made that poor ungulate sound the same as rear end. . . . In any case, I'll read this, and then I'll tell you what it is, and how it came about. "Lines from Ted: An Ars Poetica." And there's an epigraph in it, in italics, in quotes:

"Plagiarism—Good! Communism—Bad!

You can't fool anyone
You can't fool anyone that knows anything

But anything that you can use, you should use it"

—Ted Berrigan at Naropa, July '82

[Hollo reads "Lines from Ted" from *Corvus*, Minneapolis: Coffee House Press, 1995]

So. That's "Lines from Ted." And now I'll tell you how this came about. There is a footnote—in this book, I really got into footnotes. I think it's terrific to have footnotes in books of poems. Especially in books of poems that are not otherwise particularly academic. They're all in the back, so they don't interfere with the way the page looks. The note says, "The epigraph, and all the lines of this work, derive from a transcript of two workshops given by Ted Berrigan"—whose dates are 1934 through 1983—"in July 1982, at the summer session of the Jack Kerouac School of Disembodied Poetics. It is, naturally, dedicated to him, and also to the memory of Blaise Cendrars, the author of *Kodak* (and many other great works)."

I should explain that Cendrars wrote a whole book's worth of poems that he found in the pages of a very popular French adventure novelist of his time around the turn of the century, who, you know, I mean, I'm sure you've had to read or have read or have even liked to read some Victorian novelists—say Dickens, the way he describes people's clothing in detail, or other writers, I can't now think of anyone as a great example off-hand—but other writers of the period, the 19th century, when people really—that was before movies, so people really read novels, and they read them out loud to each other and so on. So people could indulge in long detailed descriptions of, say, scenery, landscape—you know, here comes a paragraph of *that*. As a kid I remember skipping those, saying to myself, "Ah-ha, I see, he's just describing a landscape again." I was an urban kid, so, the hell with it. But obviously these passages had their place in the composition. So, anyway, the guy whose name escapes me now (3) wrote a whole series of these novels, the adventures of a Dr. Cornelius. He was a definitely second-rate serial writer but he felt that since he was writing novels, after all, he had to put in some of this descriptive stuff. So he put it in, and they were a bit like James Bond novels—I mean they ranged all over the world, the Pacific, Australia, Africa, Outer Mongolia and so forth. So the guy obviously went to the encyclopedias of the time to find out what plants grew there and so forth. And they had this wonderful quality—when you looked at them—again, they were suitable for *framing*: Cendrars looked at them and framed them in his mind and said, "Hey, well, these are actually quite lovely. I mean they're complete artifacts, but if I lift them out of here and sort of put them in lines, maybe change them a little bit here and there, by God, I mean, they're like these very interesting snapshot poems!" And they were collected in a book called *Kodak*, which was a film company that Cendrars also worked for. So that explains the reference to Cendrars. In other words, Cendrars was a thief, a creative thief, and you can now—well, you can get my book *Corvus* in the bookstore, with "Lines from Ted," but you can also have the source material, it's just out—Ted Berrigan's *On the Level Every Day: Selected Talks on Poetry and the Art of Living.* The two talks that those lines came from are in there. In the poem, they are not quite in the order they are in the talks, and the poem proceeds in these sections, fourteen sections, fourteen lines, so it emulates Ted's own free form sonnet shape. Obviously, since Ted is now long gone, I could never ask him what he thought about them, but I had some reassurance and approval from his dear literary executrix and one, I think, of our greatest living poets, Alice Notley, his wife, who in a review of *Corvus* in a recent issue of *Sulfur* magazine says:

> "Lines from Ted: An Ars Poetica" is not necessarily
> Hollo's own Ars Poetica, but is probably one that
> Hollo's mind often converses with and does partake of
> from time to time. Every line in this sequence has
> Berrigan's stamp. Hollo's line arrangement expertly
> corresponds to Berrigan's syntactical pace, his delight
> in making each clause a surprise and in making Byzantine
> thought processes slowly work themselves out. "Lines
> from Ted" is an absolutely novel work.

I blush.

Uncategorizable as to author or genre, it slips out of any box one tries to fit it in.

And that's really terrific! I felt, "Lord, Thou canst let Thy servant depart in peace," you know. Because that was the intention. And I think that's the intention with doing anything like that altogether—to create works that won't fit into any convenient box. I was delighted to hear, the other night, Kevin Killian's poem composed entirely out of John Wieners lines—that was great. That was terrific. It sounded absolutely like both of them.

Again, what box would you put that in? So, I think since this is "On the Edge" week or whatever, we are, you know, we are in a sort of marginal or edge realm here. There's this line in Charles Olson, he says, I may not have it verbatim, I think it's close, "How long can a quote get / he said, eying me / with his blue eye." You know, Pound is full of quotes. If you ever travel through the *Cantos* you'll see—it's full of quotes, attributed, not attributed. So is Eliot. *The Waste Land* is a poem composed largely of quotes—again, he's a contemporary of Cendrars. And it's an idea that the late Scottish poet Hugh MacDiarmid, Scotland's cranky Neruda—I remember how back in the late fifties, early sixties, MacDiarmid was subjected to a really hilarious polemic in the pages of the *Times Literary Supplement* for having published a poem, a very lovely poem—I tried to find it, it's not in his *Selected* and I didn't pursue it any further—but a lovely short poem on some kind of animal skull on a beach that someone had discovered was a verbatim lift from some naturalist's book. (4) MacDiarmid defended himself, "Yeah, but I put it into lines, you know, and I gave it a title. Ha ha. So there." So these methods have obviously been in the air since the beginning of the century. There are quite a few other instances. I can't give you a complete bibliography of them, but I have a few more here that I'd like to show you.

Well, here's another one of my own. Let's get this ego trip over with. In my work, the *Lines from Ted* was preceded by, I think, two other instances of this kind of reframing. Or maybe three. One of them is far too long. It's sort of a kid's poem, and it was included in Jonathan Cott's anthology of poets writing for children; it's called *What Wonders in that Circle Lie*, and it's all from a great book called *"The Frog Book, North American Toads and Frogs*, with a study of the habits and life histories of those of the northeastern states, by Mary Dickerson, Doubleday Page and Company, 1906." But I won't read that.

But, God knows, thirty years ago I was asked—I was living in Iowa City at the time, and there was then as I suppose there still is now, the sort of bookshop, coffeehouse bookshop audience for poetry, and they were great fans of Charles Bukowski. And I was asked to participate in some kind of a—it wasn't a *memorial* reading, because he was still alive and kicking then, and I told the people who arranged this, I said, "Why don't you invite him? He can read his own works, no? Pass the hat or something." But no, they were going to have this reading where they all got to read Charles Bukowski works, community building, I suppose. And I couldn't quite bring myself to just pick something. I looked at his selected short stories and I saw that a great number of the sentences—understandably, since he wrote mostly in the first person singular—started with the word "I." So I just found a bunch of sentences that started with the word I, and made them into a short poem and called it *The Years*. I dedicated it to Charles Bukowski.

the years

i met her at the west end bar. i mounted.
i felt disgust & horror. i did feel some
pride. i left town. i came back. i had
some beer. i saw it. i opened the bottle
of wine. i saw it. i began to notice.
i could feel the tears. i sat there &
drank my wine. i was fairly drunk. i did
feel some pride. i could barely see. i
was a dog. i lied. i left town. i was
not a very nice fellow. i had some beer.
i came back. i walked toward the truck.
i saw it. i didn't feel it. i got up.
i began to notice. i could look out at

the people. i took my bottle. i looked.
i could barely see. i felt disgust &
horror. i opened the bottle of wine. i
had some beer. i met her at the west end
bar. i mounted. i broke her false teeth.
i was a dog. i saw it. i began to notice.
i left town. i climbed into bed. i sat
there & drank my wine. i didn't feel it.
i was a nice guy.

So that's a kind of framing. It would also at the same time be a bit of deconstruction and commentary, if you wish. I haven't read that for years, but I've had people come up to me and say things like "Oh, I just *loved* your Charles Bukowski poem—it's just *like* Charles Bukowski!" Right, right. Check. Wrong club but, you know, what can you do?

Let's see. In those two cases there was really no changing the text whatsoever—I mean, they're both selections; but there is, of course, also the question also of *erasure*, and I'm sure many of you have heard the famous story about—I'm not sure I've got the artists right here, correct me someone who knows better—Anne maybe—was it Robert Rauschenberg who gave Willem de Kooning a little painting?

ANNE WALDMAN: Yeah.

AH: It was. I got the guys right. And de Kooning decided that he would, you know, it would look a lot better—I mean, he just had the urge to erase most of it. Which —

ANNE: It was the other way around.

AH: It was the other way around: Rauschenberg felt like he should erase the de Kooning. OK. Right. Actually, it makes more sense, because Rauschenberg really is the great appropriator of images. All kinds of images—images from the news, images off television. Stuffed goats for that matter. Not live. They're stuffed, they're not alive any more, but they are the image of a goat in his work. So, yeah, erasure: there is a little-known but I think still available work of Ted Berrigan's which is a prose work, a novel called *Clear the Range*, which was created entirely by means of erasure.

ANNE: White-out.

AH: White-out, yes, yes. Wait a minute—or maybe just also felt tip pen?

ANNE: He used to have a lot of white-out.

AH: I think it's got both, actually. It's got both white-out and felt tip pen. So, several passes probably. And I don't know whether the title of the original book was—it was a Western. The original book was maybe called *Clearing the Range*, and Ted just followed dear Allen [Ginsberg]'s perennial advice to eliminate all -ings from your poetry. But I'm not sure whether it was by—was it by Luke Short? Let's just say it was Luke Short's *Clearing the Range*, it doesn't terribly matter, and Ted did a wonderful job on it. It predates—let's see, what's the publication date? It was published in '77, but I'm sure it was done before that. Probably '75. Mid-seventies. Well, it predates, or it's contemporaneous with, many of the early works produced by the L=A=N=G=U=A=G=E school, in the sense of creating an interesting new kind of non-linear narrative. And the characters in it—the main character is The Sleeper. I don't know if he arrived at his name by, you know, eraser or not, but it's a terrific idea to have a Western with the main guy's name being The Sleeper. It allows The Sleeper, obviously, to dream a lot. And the other character is Cole Younger, a historical Western character.

To give you a taste of this I'll just read a little bit from Chapter 27, and this has the kind of dialogue that violates anything. . . don't take this as a model for—well, or do. I mean, I don't know.

> At this, Cole Younger leaned forward, stiffened. The Sleeper ripped the letter across and back again.
> "Was it addressed to me?" said Cole Younger.

"Yes," said The Sleeper.

He heard a rattle in the wind.

"It was what you might call 'a letter of introduction,'" said The Sleeper. "I no use 'letters of introduction'!"

"Who from?" said Cole Younger.

"A man," said The Sleeper.

"You mean, 'Steve'?" said Cole Younger.

The Sleeper hesitated. He did not wish to think.

"Well," he said, "it was Steve."

"Steve knows about me and other men," said Cole Younger. "I take opinion. Did he recommend you to me?"

"Of course," said The Sleeper.

"How long did he know you?" said Cole Younger.

"One minute," said The Sleeper.

"That's about five minutes in the life of most men," said Cole Younger.

"That's true," said The Sleeper.

"I like you," said Cole Younger. "Show me his letter."

"I read that letter," said The Sleeper. "It was boring."

"What did it say?" said Cole Younger.

"It was about me," said The Sleeper.

"Who?" said Cole Younger.

"Me," said The Sleeper.

"Go on," said The Sleeper.

"I take it that you want to go to sleep," said Cole Younger.

"That's the idea," said The Sleeper.

"But why?" said Cole Younger.

"Take it easy," said The Sleeper.

"It's not an easy life," said Cole Younger. "It's a fat life."

"I may look fat, but I'm not," said The Sleeper.

"I see," said Cole Younger.

The Sleeper yawned.

It's all like that, you know. It's a really good read.
I mean you probably shouldn't—it's not a bedtime read, really,

because it'll wake you up, and you'll want to read, if you have anyone next to you, want to read sections from it, and you'll both have the giggles. And get the wrong kinds of brainwaves going.

Another famous literary work achieved by means of erasure is John Ashbery's poem *Europe*, from a collection called *The Tennis Court Oath* that many feel—particularly younger readers and cohorts, colleagues— is one of Ashbery's most interesting collections, but that I gather he himself has been somewhat ambivalent about in later years. I mean it's not one that Helen Vendler would like. I'm not saying John is buddying up to Helen Vendler, but, well, so what? They both live in New York.

In any case, *Europe* is a longish poem in many little numbered parts. It's over a hundred—111 parts, and it was created, again, by a similar method of erasure of a kid's book. Well, not a kid's book but I guess what do they call it? A young adult—juvenile book—called *Beryl and Her Biplane*, written sometime in the 1920s, when people really still had biplanes for one thing, and it was very adventurous for persons called Beryl to fly them. And so it is a completely wonderful mysterious work, where here and there Ashbery sort of gives you a hint that this is indeed a, you know, found work with erasures. In section 8, which is terrific actually—well, I should read section 7 before that, because part of it again is in the framing:

> What might have
>   children singing
> the horses
>   the seven
> breaths under tree, fog
> clasped—absolute, unthinking
> menace to our way of life.
> uh unearth more cloth
> This could have been done —
> This could not be done

So completely mysterious, you know. Sort of a bit like a Joe Ceravolo poem. Now, section number eight:

In the falling twilight of the wintry afternoon all
looked dull and cheerless. The car stood outside with
Ronald Pryor and Collins attending to some slight engine
trouble—the fast, open car which Ronnie sometimes
used to such advantage. It was covered with mud, after
the long run from Suffolk, for they had started from
Harbury long before daylight, and, until an hour ago,
had been moving swiftly up the Great North Road by way
of Stanford, Grantham and Duncaster to York. There they
had turned away to Ripon, where, for an hour, they had
eaten and rested. In a basket the waiter had placed
some cold food with some bread and a bottle of wine, and
this had been duly transferred to the car.

All was now ready for the continuance of the journey.

So that's the raw material there. That's just, "Vroom!" That's just like
leaving it in there. And then, 9:

> The decision in his life
> soul elsewhere
> the gray hills
> out there on the road darkness
> covering lieutenant
>
> there is a cure

So it shifts in and out of these. . .but it mostly stays in this latter mode.
Section 49:

> I'm on my way to Hull
>
> grinned the girl

And so on. It's too long to read—I'd love to read the whole thing. I've
never read it aloud to anyone, but you can find it in the library.

Other instances—well, there's one more instance of erasure. I mean erasure and combination. Jeffrey Robinson, who is a professor of English at the University of Colorado, and is a poet as well, a year or two ago published this book called *Romantic Presences*, a very worthwhile scholarly book on Wordsworth and Shelley. But then appended to this— and he's written a bunch of these, he has more than what he's got in the book—appended is a little section of poems of "his" in which he links words from the great Romantic poets to words from contemporary, more or less contemporary 20th century poets like Paul Celan, Lorine Niedecker, Robert Lowell, Blaise Cendrars, Charles Reznikoff. He's got one—oh, maybe I should read this one. Keats and Adrienne Rich. Number 15. Let's see. Far out. Oh, yeah. So, this is erasure and combination:

> fears
> wintry fears—
> Is it self or
> language itself
> that may cease to be —
> of scraping egg crust in
> a high romance
>
> abortion in the bowl
> an hour that ice spits
> its fair creature
>
> the ceasing of *you*
> I am receding
> the vanishing point
> the period to which
> all sentences teem
> in a house on the shore
> where the poet and the
> dumb abortion woman
> cease to cease

One with Celan, Wordsworth and Paul Celan:

slowsound, timestrange
issue forth
—and still fainter —
      the first pale stars

No voice
      perchance

Bernadette Mayer in her—and I hope you're taking notes of all these names because, you know, that's what lectures are—lectures are namedropping. One of my little—you know I have these little invisible crows that sit on my shoulders and travel around and overhear things, and after Bob Creeley's as I thought wonderful lecture and reading here, one of them had heard someone who I don't think necessarily is—may just—probably was just a visitor from the outside, had heard her say, "Oh, gosh, all this *namedropping*—who does he think he is?" Well, he thinks he is probably Robert Creeley, and namedropping, for crissakes—you know, if you're going to talk about writing and literature and po-etry, there will be *names*. These things don't come out of the air. You know, if you want to turn around and talk about the Inner Sibling—hear a talk about the Inner Sibling, then, sure, that's somebody else, but you won't get that here. I mean you can talk—you can just say one word—Grimm. Or two words—the brothers Grimm and Carl Gustav Jung are the only two names that need be mentioned in that talk—that other talk. [Growls inaudibly.]

Where was I? Bernadette Mayer, in her lovely list of things to do when the muses do not descend or stop descending or maybe never descended on you, if you're not—if you don't work that way—she has a list of over a hundred various strategies to get the *kavyayantra*, the poetry machine going. And one of them is, in fact, to take either a poem you love or a poem you hate—don't take a poem that you're indifferent to—and go through it, line by line—*answer* each line. You might want to type it out so that there's space between the lines, then you answer the first line, and then you answer the second line or add to it or continue it, whatever you want to do, and then you take out the original poem and see what you've got. That's partly erasure, but you've also got something that you may feel came out of your very own personal affect—not that your personal affect doesn't enter into what you find and arrange or erase—but, you know, same nouns, different story.

Obviously this raises questions in our minds about such things as originality. We haven't really discussed that much so far this summer, I don't think. In terms of literary, historical, and critical and theoretical sensibility it's an outmoded concept. What's "original?" Certainly anything made out of words is—unless you invent the substance in which you create something—let's put it this way: if you're the inventor of some new kind of plastic and make a sculpture out of that material, then *maybe* that's "original." But, you know, paint, bronze, plaster, whatever it is, words, you know, they're *there*, and we're inside of all that stuff. We contain that stuff, but we're also just inside of it. So it was a notion—I guess it was a notion favored by the 19th century, a notion that goes very well with rising bourgeoisie capitalism—the bourgeois wants to know whether what he or she is *buying* is "original." Is this an *original* Rubens, not a copy? Another name I'd like to drop now is Walter Benjamin, Austrian essayist and critic, died in the turmoil of World War II, committed suicide in fact. But he has an essay on *Art in the Age of Reproduction* that's worth checking out. (5) He still definitely struggled, but in a very intelligent way, with these notions of the original and the copy and the reproduction. Now of course most of our images are reproductions. I mean we're inundated by reproduced images. And there's a photographer, I can't remember her name—I asked Jane and she couldn't either—but there's a photographer who takes photographs of old photographs —

STUDENT: Sherri Levine.

AH: Sherri Levine. Yeah. Photographs of old photographs. To literally take a photograph of a photograph is very interesting—because photographs are, by their nature, I mean not that paintings aren't too—but photographs are far more perishable. Unless they're kept in the dark, literally, they will fade. And black and white lasts a lot longer, or sepia, the old kinds of prints last much longer. Color photographs—some of you may already have had that experience: your baby pictures are a very odd kind of sort of bluish-green, mostly. They fade. But to take a reproduction of something that in a sense is already a reproduction, that's really a hall of mirrors. That's really quite terrific. So, anyway, I won't go into that. I mean The Original and The Genius and The Muse have sort of moved into Madame Tussaud's Wax Museum by now. And we may visit them there and have fun with them once in a while.

I hope it's obvious that I am not advocating "plagiarism." There is somebody—there is a rather low-key sort of poet who I think is also a doctor—names, forget about names, yeah, if I could remember all the names then I'd *really* be dropping names. (6) But he's written a book about someone else plagiarizing his poems—you know, this was in the great subterranean world of little magazines, which you will soon enter too, no doubt. Well, no, it's not such a bad place. It's a big place—it's large. But it's so large, in fact, that this guy had been published, had been publishing for about ten years, he'd been publishing his works in one sector of the little poetry magazine flora, and somebody else had literally just lifted his poems, and put his name to them, and published them in some other sector of the map. And it took the man years to discover this. So now he got a chance to write a book about this, and to publish some of his poems in it. He hired a detective—by God, it brought some adventure into his life! That was obviously interesting as a conceptual situation, but looking at the originals it was a little hard to imagine why a) anyone would want to steal them, and b) why anyone would want to publish them. But they were published. Twice. So go figure.

Let's see, what did I possibly want to wind up with? Well, John Ashbery, talking about his poem *Europe*—Harry Mathews, a very interesting poet and fiction writer, associated with that group, an old friend of Ashbery's and Kenneth Koch's and Frank O'Hara's and James Schuyler's, is also a member of the French *Oulipo*—an acronym for *Ouvroir de la Littérature Potentielle*—the "Workshop for Potential Literature." It's a group that's been going for over 20 years now and he, I think, is the only American member. It was founded by the poet Raymond Queneau and a couple of mathematicians, actually, with an interest in literature. It's a group that studies the structures of writing and in a sense is interested in—it's *formalism* in that old 1920's real true sense, not like when we now hear about the "New Formalists." People like Mayakovsky, who was a formalist associated with painters and critics and so on, who were interested in what forms in the arts are, and where they come from, and what you can do with them, and what would a new form be, and so forth. So Mathews has been very inventive in these ways, and one of his—this is a little essay called "Mathews's Algorithm," which is too long to go into in detail here. I may go into it in my workshop next week, because it does relate—interestingly enough, it relates very much to the sonnet. But he says, "Using existent material"—which is basically what we've been talking about or what I've been trying to talk about here:

> Using existent material, returning to Shakespeare. Take
> 14 of his best known sonnets. Arrange the verses of
> each sonnet horizontally so as to form a set and
> superimpose the set. After a shift left, here is the
> first of the fourteen possible readings.

Slightly edited as to punctuation, but otherwise, you know, every word by the Bard.

> Shall I compare thee to a summer's day
> And dig deep trenches in thy beauty's field
> Why loves thou that which thou receives not gladly
> Bare ruined choirs where late the sweet birds sang
> Anon permit the basest clouds to ride
> And do whatever thou wilt, swift-footed time.
> Nor Mars his sword nor war's quick fire shall burn
> Even such a beauty as you, master now.
> Love's not time's full, though rosy lips and cheeks
> When other petty griefs have done their spite
> And heavily, for vow to vow tell o'er
> That time will come and take my love away
> For thy sweet love remembered such wealth brings
> As any she belied beyond compare.

Shakespeare. Right. And you could make at least fourteen more of these. And people have done so, so don't do it again.

And I want to mention one of my favorite prose writers, Frederic Tuten. They recently reissued a book of his, it's a novel, called *The Adventures of Mao on the Long March*. Which contains—he didn't, in the first edition, give the sources, and they're interesting but they're not in any sense essential to the work in terms of—you don't *have to* know. But there are borrowings from Shakespeare, Jack London, Hawthorne, John William de Forest (author of *Miss Ravenel's Conversion*), Mao, of course, Melville, Cooper—James Fenimore Cooper, Emerson, Friedrich Engels, Washington Irving, Walter Pater, John Ruskin, and Oscar Wilde in this book, which is a novel about the adventures of Mao on the Long March. He's a delightful writer. This was his first novel and perhaps artier than the others, but I highly recommend Tuten to your attention. There's one called *Tallien*—a character from the French Revolution—*Tallien, a Brief Romance.* And *Tin-Tin in the New World*—Tin-Tin, a French comic strip much loved by kids over there, and I guess over here, too. And the most recent one: *Van Gogh's Bad Cafe*. Terrific writer.

Now then, I think we're approaching wind-up and question time. I think we'll combine those two. So take a deep breath, do your stretches, whatever. I may light a cigarette and pop in and out and we'll have the questions. I see a hand rise back there. Please come to the microphone. Right? Brian wants you to—wants you at the microphone.

STUDENT: (unintelligible)

AH: You've changed your mind? Well, maybe you'll change it back again. There were a couple of hands up here—

STUDENT: This is a quick question. I was just. . . I wondered who it was that wrote the *Romantic Presences?*

AH: Romantic presences?

STUDENT: *Romantic Presences*, the one where you —

AH: Oh, *Romantic Presences*. Jeffrey Robinson.

STUDENT: Jeffrey?

AH: Jeffrey. Yeah. Jeffrey with a J. J-E-F-F-R-E-Y. Cole?

COLE SWENSEN: I just wanted to mention two eraser books that I think are really interesting experiments, and one combines with the Harry Mathews also. And that's Stephen Ratcliffe's book *Where Late the Sweet Birds Sang*. And I think it's an O book. (7)

AH: I think so too. I don't know that one. I know—I like Steve's work very much actually.

COLE: He takes, I don't how many Shakespearean sonnets and whites-out or erases whole sections, so that you get a wonderful spacing as well as this fragmentation. And the other one I wanted to mention is Tom Phillips's book, *A Humument*.

AH: But of course. But of course! Yes!

COLE: Which is wonderful.

AH: I have all the editions of that. It's an extraordinary book.

COLE: Why don't you describe it briefly?

AH: Well, would you like to describe it? No? OK. British artist Tom Phillips who came across a two—I think it's two volumes, although in some editions it's just one big fat volume, a novel. . .Victorian novel, again, (8) now source material, called *A Human Document*, which must rival the *Book of Mormon* for being the most boring—please, I hope I'm not offending anybody. I mean, I'm quoting Mark Twain here, who said that the *Book of Mormon* was a work of genius because to write something *that* boring you really had to be a genius. But *A Human Document* comes close, you know. It's very moralistic, dry as dust, tedious. . .tedious. . .I mean I can't imagine. . .it's the kind of book—certainly we can all imagine reading Dickens, or Balzac or, you know, Eugene Sue, or Rafael Sabatini, God knows. . .but this is *unimaginable*. It's unimaginable that anyone. . .But it was a big success in its day. I think that was due to sadistic fathers who liked to read things out loud, who would force their oppressed families to listen to them read it after dinner.

But in any case, he found it, Tom Phillips did, and he obviously realized all of that. I mean, anyone in their right mind would. But he also saw that it was thousands and thousands of *words*, and he decided to go through it methodically, page by page, and leave only the words that might make some kind of interesting sense next to each other. To leave only those words on the page. That's not very many, in most cases. There's usually only a few, and they're usually not next to each other on the same line either. And he would circle those and join them together so they would say something, and then make the rest of the page a painting. So it's a lovely book. It's available in paperback. It's called *A Humument*. It's a Thames and Hudson paperback. It's not even that expensive. I think it's about eleven bucks. It's gone through several editions, and it's full-color, and really fun to read. It's also fun to look at because the pages are real paintings. But the original print of the book shows through in places, just as a ghost, so there's this ghostly screen in back of things. And. . .pardon?

STUDENT: (unintelligible)

AH: When did he do this? When did he start it? It's a lifelong project. He's still working on it. I think he started it in the late sixties. I mean, he's done other things. That's not all he does. But he has marvelous projects. He has things like taking pictures of, and then painting, the same nondescript sort of street corner in North London at ten-year intervals. Tom Phillips is definitely a master. He also has a translation, a pretty good translation of Dante's "Inferno" illustrated by himself which was actually remaindered. It was remaindered. It was still 35 dollars but worth every penny.

Any more questions? Ideas? Suggestions? Wishes, Lies, and Dreams? (9)

I was thinking one sort of epigraph to all this could obviously be what the great German poet and playwright Bertolt Brecht said: "In matters of intellectual property I have always been a bit lax." His famous "Threepenny Opera" is essentially a creative translation of "The Beggar's Opera" by John Gay. He just moves it a couple of centuries forward. A lot of his poetry is versions of François Villon, and so on. And he combined that with being a Socialist. He combined that with some political sense that no one really has a right to insist that you cannot use their stuff. Although he did actually get into trouble during his exile; during the Hitler period in World War II he was on the run, and he spent some time in Sweden, some time in Finland, and quite a few years in L.A. And during his time in Finland, he befriended or was befriended by a Finnish, actually Estonian-born woman, a playwright, Hella Wuolijoki, who had written a number of plays. Like most people of that generation in those parts, she was fluent in German. So she told Brecht the stories of her plays. And he enjoyed hearing them. And one of them in particular took his fancy, which, as it turns out, is an ancient story—I mean she got it from folklore—native Finnish folklore—but apparently it does go back to Babylon.

I'll tell you in a minute what it is. He liked the idea, and he made a few suggestions to her—this was one she was still working on—and then he decided to. . . I think he first of all decided to translate it, but with the help—he didn't have any Finnish—but with the help of someone else he knew, and he got so enamored of the tale of this play—that he wrote his own play based on it. In English it is known as *Mr. Puntila and His Hired Hand Matti*. And, you know, it's a version of—apparently the first time that this story was recorded was in Babylon. It's the story of the Master and the Slave where the Master is the really, you know, harsh master. But when he gets drunk on weekends, he gets very lonely, and he invites the Slave to come and have a drink with him, and as the evening wears on, he gets more and more liberal and friendly and humanitarian, and he promises the Slave, he says "Oh, yes, as of tomorrow, you'll have your own cottage, and you know I've been thinking about setting you free anyway" and gets really chummy with him and has little adventures with him and stuff. But come Monday, man, he's *back*. He's sober, and he's grim, and he doesn't remember a word of that stuff. That's the basic plot. So, in a sense, who owns that? That's as old as what we jokingly call mankind. Yeah?

STUDENT: I was wondering if you're familiar with Jerzy Kosinski's last book, *The Hermit of 69th Street*.

AH: That's one I haven't read.

STUDENT: It's very interesting. It's about fifty per cent his own text, and then for various effects throughout he'll insert a line from Conrad, go on with his own text, you know, a paragraph from Einstein's introduction to the theory of relativity, then some more of his own text, footnoted, you know, see this book about kings of Poland in the 900s, and very interesting.

AH: Well, that's a dialogue, right. That's having a conversation.

STUDENT: (unintelligible, but apparently a question concerning acknowledgment of source material)

AH: Yeah, it's a good idea to, unless, you know, the material has been so transformed. . . And that's another thing—I could go on talking about translation and transformation—a whole further field adjoining this one. But yes, it's a very good idea to credit what you use—as it would be in your paper, you know. Say "I got this off the Internet." Just kidding.

STUDENT: A couple of years ago, there was a reprint of a book that came out and I think it was called *Void*, maybe. And I can't remember the author's name, but the entire book is written without the letter e.

AH: Oh, oh. Georges Perec. *A Void*. Yes, another member of the *Oulipo* group. Sadly gone now, but a terrific writer.

STUDENT: So I was wondering how placing limitations on yourself with the writing affects the—like the practice you're talking about?

AH: Well, I think we—no matter what, we have limitations, you know? I mean we are within limits, one hopes, anyway. It's a risky thing not to be. But sure, I think it helps. I think it absolutely helps. I mean it's what's made millions of people write rhyming verse, for instance. It's— say, well the next line or the one after that has to end the way this one just ended: that's a very simplistic limitation, but obviously the more you can invent of those, the more—and obviously some of them have been overused, so you don't want to use those. I think the tradition of this school, the Jack Kerouac School, sort of goes with William Carlos Williams' impatience with iambic pentameter, for instance. Which is not to say. . . it's quite easy to write. I mean, just try talking with an English accent and you've got your iambic pentameter.

STUDENT: In some ways this seems like a natural lead from what you've been talking about, but no one's mentioned, using your own work, doing the erasure combination or stealing from your own work— such as what you've written before, or two pieces that you've been working on separately. I don't know if you can comment on your experience with that?

AH: Oh, absolutely. In fact, the same book that has the *Lines from Ted* sequence in it, has two works of mine that were created that way, that go back to much earlier work. My intention wasn't to abolish the earlier work but to play with it—you know, to see what's there, and what would I now like to do with it. And it involved quite a bit of erasure and rearrangement.

Well, I think now we have a Women's Student Panel coming up, I seem to remember. Yes?

STUDENT: (unintelligible)

AH: Pardon me? All right. So, thank you.

Kerouac School summer session, 26 June 1997
Transcribed by Randy Roark, edited by AH

Notes

1 "We are like dwarfs on the shoulders of giants."—Bernard of Chartres, 12th century CE; "If I have seen further it is by standing on the shoulders of giants."—Sir Isaac Newton, 1675. (Thanks to Randy Roark for these references.)
2 The title is "L.H.O.O.Q," which in French phonetically reproduces the phrase "Elle a chaud au cul" ("Her ass feels hot").
3 Gustave Le Rouge (1867-1938). "The plagiarism was 'discovered' by Francis Lacassin in 1966, but twenty years earlier Cendrars had already given it away [. . .] writing that he had been cruel enough to show an (unnamed) volume of poems to Le Rouge which he had scissor-and-pasted out of the latter's adventure novels. [. . .] the 'finding' of this poetry never ridicules its source or its dissimulated author." Ron Padgett, in his introduction to *Blaise Cendrars: Complete Poems, translated by Ron Padgett*, Berkeley, University of California Press 1992.
4 The poem:

Perfect

On the Western Seaboard of South Uist
(Los muertos abren los ojos a los que viven)

I found a pigeon's skull on the machair,
All the bones pure white and dry, and chalky,
But perfect,
Without a crack or flaw anywhere.

At the back, rising out of the beak,
Were twin domes like bubbles of thin bone,

Almost transparent, where the brain had been
That fixed the tilt of the wings.

(From *Hugh MacDiarmid: Selected Poems*, New Directions 1986.)

It was not extracted from a naturalist's work, but from a short story by the Welsh author Glyn Jones. The Spanish epigraph can be read "The dead open the eyes of those who live" or "The dead open their eyes *on* those who live."

5   The essay appears in Benjamin's collection *Illuminations*.
6   E.G. Burrows.
7   O Books, Leslie Scalapino's poetry press.
8   The author is W. H. Mallock.
9   Reference to the title of a book by Kenneth Koch about writing poetry with children.

A few further examples of related methods used in some of my own work:

I   RE-CONTEXTUALIZATION

"Wasp Sex Myth" (1) and "Wasp Sex Myth" (2) in *Sojourner Microcosms: New & Selected Poems 1959-1977* (Berkeley, Blue Wind Press, 1977). Here, the materials were gleaned from a book called *The Sensuous Woman*. Also see "footnote poem" to those two works, "How I Composed Some of My Items" in *Near Miss Haiku: praises laments aphorisms reports* (Chicago, Yellow Press, 1990).

"The Anima Abstract" in *Sojourner Microcosms* uses material from Cornelia Brunner's essay *Die Anima als Schicksalsproblem des Mannes* (credited at end of text). A possibly not entirely successful recontextualization, since some readers seem to have read it as a 'straight' didactic text, missing the flavor of Jungian absurdity I intended to convey.

2   APPROPRIATION/ALTERATION

Section within quotation marks in "Down & Up" in *Sojourner Microcosms*. The quote is from James Dickey's introduction to Paul Carroll's anthology *New Young American Poets*. I substituted the word "kelp" for the word "poetry."

"In Annie's Garden: after & with Guillaume Apollinaire" in *Finite Continued*. A semantically quite 'close' translation of Apollinaire's 1901 poem, which, however, highlights the various kinds of chauvinism evident in the original ("many's the time I broke my cane / on the back of some dumb peasant" and "that time you surprised me sticking my tongue /into a working-class redhead's mouth").

3   TEXTS COMPOSED BY QUASI-'OULIPIAN' DEVICES

"Songs of the Sentence Cubes" in *No Complaints* (Toothpaste Press, 1983). Poems composed by means of a game, "Sentence Cubes," similar to the currently available "Poetry for Your Table" or "Magnetic Poetry Kit." It consisted of words inscribed on the sides of plastic or wooden cubes.

"Minigolf" in *Outlying Districts* (Coffee House Press, 1990). The titles and motifs of this sequence (*The Way; Castle; Pinball; Alligator; Elephant; Pygmy Hut; Around the World; Hills; The Jump; Rocket; Glance; Champ; Lighthouse; The Curve; Snail; Tic-Toc; Chicken Coop; The Fish*) derive from a game of "minigolf" my wife Jane and I played one afternoon in '88 somewhere between New Orleans and Biloxi. A headnote to the sequence reads: "Anselm kept the scorecard and named poems written during the remainder of the year after each obstacle on the course—thus, 'Minigolf', sporadically annotated, became a kind of record of the Game of that Year."

"Not a Form at All but a State of Mind" in *Corvus* is a sequence of twelve fourteen-line poems consisting of original lines and scrupulously footnoted quotes arranged in an hour-glass pattern, fanning out from the middle. Individual lines acquire new neighbors and resonances through out the work, which, in a sense, is an *hommage* both to Raymond Queneau's ten billion poems (or however many there are) and to John Taggart's marvelous fugal works.

4   "COMPUTER-ASSISTED" GENERATION

To some extent, "Lines from Ted, Not a Form. . .", and "Reviewing the Tape: i.m. Piero Heliczer" (in *Corvus*) could be regarded as "computer-assisted" in the sense that their creation would have been far more labor-intensive without my Mac. "Reviewing the Tape" consists of lines culled from *Sojourner Microcosms* arranged into a sequence of seven 'sonnets,' a temporary retrospective distillate of my work of the years 1959-77.

Some Thoughts for a Celebration of Robert Creeley, and Black Mountain, on the Island of Mallorca

1

THE INVITATION TO PARTICIPATE in this event came as a delightful surprise at the midpoint of a sojourn in a small village near Paris, at an artists' and writers' retreat located in an old hotel once patronized by Irish, Scottish, and Scandinavian poets and painters, Robert Louis Stevenson, Frank O'Meara, and August Strindberg among them.

I had been pondering one of the several projects assigned to me, by myself and others, to be undertaken in the five months granted to me in that hospitable place: an entry on the "Troubadours" for an encyclopedia of poetry edited by poet Ron Padgett and designed for the use of high school and college students. I had been wondering (still am, as no doubt many before me) how the troubadours "did it," how they managed to live and work their dream of Congruence—of the joining of sound and sense, poetry and music, love and desire, belief and doubt—how could they maintain this in a world surely every bit as *in*congruent, irrational, and random as ours?

And thus, when I received the surprising invitation to participate in this event, I immediately 'flashed' on the fact that one of the books Robert Creeley published in Mallorca from his Divers Press in 1953 was Paul Blackburn's *Proensa*, a slim volume of a dozen translations from the Occitan masters of *trobar.* There it was, a connection—and connections, I suspect, is what we poets mostly live by, even in our postmodern skepticism toward notions of coherence and spiritual congruence. We make connections; we recognize them when they are made for us (Jungians call this synchronicity), and we delight in them when they become lasting associations.

I'm not sure if I ever owned a copy of that early Provençal book—books have habits of coming and going, just like people—but I do still have, although not with me in France, one or two Divers Press items, including the poems of Katue Kitasono, Ezra Pound's Japanese correspondent, and an issue of the Black Mountain Review. Gael Turnbull, an early friend in England, gave me a copy of Creeley's *The Whip*, and his *A Form of Women* was a glorious find in the Better Books bookstore in London's Charing Cross Road—an almost daily stop on my way home from Bush House where I worked for the BBC from 1958 through 1967.

During those years, that book shop and one or two others provided a genuine if somewhat erratic pipeline to small U.S.American presses and magazines—Jonathan Williams' Jargon Press, Ted Wilentz's Totem/Corinth Books, Andrew Hoyem's and Dave Haselwood's Auerhahn Press, Lawrence Ferlinghetti's City Lights Pocket Poets.

In some recent correspondence about critical attempts at literary groupings, chronologies, 'lineages,' Tom Raworth reminded me that he and I, as well as Lee Harwood, Roy Fisher, Ian Hamilton Finlay, Harry Fainlight, and a number of other UK poets, received these gifts from across the Atlantic all by ourselves, i.e. without any academic intermediaries. There was no friendly professor waving a copy of *For Love* or *Howl* at us and saying, hey, you should read this! The only one among us with academic affiliation was Michael Horovitz who was working on a Joyce thesis at Oxford but otherwise was seriously engaged in staging poetry and jazz road shows in a spirit of Dada Revival.

I remember one occasion in particular that illustrates the contrast between academia and the literary arts as I was experiencing them. Mike had invited Bob Creeley, on one of his first visits to London, to read at one of the multifaceted events he was organizing. The venue was a basement dive in Soho, and Bob and I sat through the various offerings, which included a young woman in a bikini halter and leopard skin tights doing some sort of expressionist jazz dance number. If memory serves, this was the point at which Bob became a little nervous about, as it were, "fitting in," but went on to acquit himself admirably with a heartstopping rendition of *The Ballad of the Despairing Husband*.

But what was it, exactly, that Tom Raworth, myself, and others discovered in pages of the *Black Mountain Review*, Amiri Baraka's *Yugen*,

Cid Corman's *Origin*? Even though the exact chronology has grown a bit hazy in memory, I think I can safely say that this new work from the United States was exciting, perplexing, and inspiring in entirely new ways—tilted in directions that the writing found in contemporary *British* books and journals had never come close to. In 1960, the publication of Donald M. Allen's anthology *The New American Poetry 1945-1960* made the fact of this transatlantic renaissance even more real, and, for better or worse, it also instituted the categories into which its various strands were then classified: Beat, Black Mountain, 'West Coast', New York School.

Almost half a century later, the categories are no longer so clearly delineated. It seems to me that the younger generations of U.S.American cultural workers in poetry and poetics see "The New American Poetry" as the mainstream of post-World War Two second-wave modernism, and there is quite a bit of dissension among them as to whether they should consider themselves as continuing that lineage or declare themselves staunchly *post*-modernist. But I am happy to leave such arguments to those who enjoy them.

As a young man coming of age in the European aftermath of World War II, I found in the work of the New American Poets, and in Creeley's poetry in particular, a spirit that was welcoming, challenging, and curiously familiar to my own 'rootless cosmopolitan' post-war sensibility. In his *ABC of Reading*, Pound says "The man who really knows can tell all that is transmissible in a very few words." The 'few words' of Creeley's poems hit home with an unrivaled accuracy of transmission. Their weave, both plain and ironic, is always aware of how insecure the ground of language can be. Their sense of humor, in the widest application of that idea, is existentially *noir* as well as humane: light flashing through dark trees by the side of the road.

Mind and heart stop for a fractional moment, time slows, then Thelonious strikes the next note. And the next. And you wonder how you could, ever, not have known that this would be the next word—so unexpected, yet perfect.

But you didn't know, or you forgot, and the poem's music takes you through a series of the kind of observations that, in Pound's words, "rest as the enduring data of philosophy"—a love of the kind of wisdom that refuses to abandon the endlessly and even exasperatingly contradictory human heart for grand abstractions.

2

Drive, he said. And years later, no longer in swinging London but in the great monstrous USA, we're on our way from Baton Rouge Louisiana where, after causing a bit of righteous ruckus at the local institution of football and learning (in that order), we get so weary of our disgruntled hosts that we do not want to stay another minute and decide to *drive* back instead of waiting for the morning plane, drive all the way back to Buffalo New York, first heading the wrong way, west instead of east, this can't be right, look at all that Spanish moss, and make it through hours of talk and laughter and blizzards, on our way, on the road, reminiscing about earlier considerably shorter road trip in darkest Michigan, we got there then, wherever that was, and we'll make it this time too.

As we do one morning in Gloucester, years before, when Bob's trusty old VW bug comes to a halt on the beach and sinks into soft wet sand up to its hubcaps, whereupon one of our company proceeds to walk into the waves, heading east toward the rising sun, and has to be rescued before the waters close above her head, she is a tall woman but not that tall, and then we all trudge to the nearest general store for some terrible coffee and a telephone.

I think back on such moments as instances of the U.S.American *duende*. Which is all about distances, about getting there, and the there never quite turning out the way one had imagined, or there not even being any *there* there, but instead, something else both comical and vaguely or even overtly threatening, yet again, at times, unexpectedly beautiful and reaffirming—as in *Histoire de Florida:*

Miles and miles of space are here in unexpected senses,

sky washed with clouds, changing light, long sunsets

sinking across water and land, air that freshens, intimate.
Endless things growing, all horizontal, an edge, a rise only of feet

above the sea's surface, or the lakes, the ponds, the rivers,
all out, nothing that isn't vulnerable, no depths, no rooted senses
other than the actual fabric of roots, skin of survivals.

3

Contemporary French poet and art critic Alain Jouffroy recently remi-
nisced about something Marcel Duchamp pointed out to him many
moons ago: "[. . .] since posterity changes its criteria of taste and judg-
ment every fifty years or so, no one can stake any advance claims on its
support without exposing themselves to ridicule." Jouffroy has also spoken "in favor of the dissenting role of an avant-garde made up of individuals whose interconnections exist outside any political, institutional
or commercial system," and called "this system of direct relations between individuals [the] Externet." (Interview by Jacques Henric, *artpress*
238, September 1998, Paris.)

Yet, such an "externet," an association of artists, poets, philosophers,
human beings whose connections are as far as humanly possible "outside any political, institutional or commercial system," does not, as far
as I can see, require its participants to be apolitical, a-institutional, or
even a a-commercial. To glance back at the troubadours: on one hand,
they can be seen as workers in the "arts-and-entertainment" industry
of their day; on the other, as victims of a political repression that struck
many of them and their people very severely in the Albigensian cru-
sade. The second wave of modernist poets—in the United States as
well as in post-World War II central Europe—responded to absolutist
systems and their consequences and agreed with Sartre's dictum that
the artist's role must always be anti-authoritarian, no matter how seemingly benign the authority. In the case of The New American Poets,
their work, as it appeared in Don Allen's anthology, and before that, in
the Black Mountain Review and a plethora of individual small press

volumes, can certainly be seen as part of the intellectual and political awareness that built up the head of steam leading to the lid blowing off in 1968 on both sides of the Atlantic. Yet again, as with the troubadours, an understanding of their work *only* in those terms would be an over-simplification.

Skeptic and agnostic though I am, I find myself in intuitive agreement with Scottish poet Ian Hamilton Finlay when he says that "consecutive sentences are the beginning of the secular".... . Not to introduce notions of the "sacred" or "numinous" here, I also feel that I could go on uttering many more "consecutive sentences," trying to express my sense of what it is that generates and holds together our temporal webs of poetic understanding and solidarity, without getting any closer to succeeding even half as well as Creeley does in these lines from his poem *The Company:*

> [. . .]
> Recorders ages hence will look for us
> not only in books, one hopes, nor only under rocks
> but in some common places of feeling,
> small enough—but isn't the human
>
> just that echoing, resonant edge
> of what it knows it knows,
> takes heart in remembering
> only the good times, yet
>
> can't forget whatever it was,
> comes here again, fearing this
> is the last day, this is the last,
> the last, the last.

François Villon, who took up some of the Occitanian poets' forms a few centuries later and set them well to his own music, was another who lived on that "echoing, resonant edge / of what it knows it knows." In *The Spirit of Romance*, Pound says about *him*:

Villon never forgets his fascinating, revolting self. If, however, he sings the song of himself he is, thank God, free from that horrible air of rectitude with which Whitman rejoices in being Whitman. Villon's song is selfish through self-absorption; he does not, as Whitman, pretend to be conferring a philanthropic benefit on the race by recording his own self-complacency.

Not entirely fair, of course, and as we know, Pound later "made his peace" with Walt. But in a world where much baser versions of a "horrible air of rectitude" and self-complacency still run rampant in what passes for public discourse, voices like Villon's and Creeley's thankfully still create a common space in which there is room to breathe—in which there are human *Presences* (one of my favorite Creeley works), places of feeling, light on the waves, light flashing through dark trees by the side of the road.

Grez-sur-Loing
September 1998

from **Where If Not Here**

give up your ampersands & lowercase 'i's
they still won't like you
the bosses of official verse culture
(U.S. Branch)   but kidding aside
I motored off that map a long time ago
yet have old friends
still happily romping in the English lyric
and Reverdy! dear Reverdy! so much of him rhymes
it must be   *poésie   ma chérie*. . .
looks at the stacks of books on the floor
gods help us, dear poets
pass the salt pass the mustard
hike the present
or the hypothetically honest horse-drawn past

colophon

Set in **Janson**, based on a face cut by
Hungarian Miklós Kis (1650-1702) during
his craftsman days in Amsterdam, but
wrongly attributed to Anton Janson, Dutch
typefounder and contemporary of Kis.
This version adapted for Linotype by
Hermann Zapf in 1952. It shows a
well-proportioned balance between
ascenders and descenders with
a Baroque delight in the colorful
contrast of thick and thin strokes:
old style, zesty usefulness,
fit and hale.

•

Book design by J. Bryan

ANSELM HOLLO was born in 1934 in Helsinki, Finland, and was educated there and in the U.S. (senior year in high school on an exchange scholarship). In his early twenties, he left Finland to live and work as a writer and translator, first in Germany and Austria, then in London, where he was employed by the BBC's European Services in their Finnish Program from 1958 to 1967. For the last thirty-two years, Hollo has lived in the United States, teaching creative writing and literary translation at numerous colleges and universities, including SUNY Buffalo, The University of Iowa, and The University of Colorado. He has read his work, lectured, and conducted workshops at universities and colleges, art museums and galleries, literary conferences, coffeehouses, and living rooms.

He is now on the faculty of the Jack Kerouac School of Poetics, the graduate Writing and Poetics department at The Naropa Institute, a Buddhist-inspired nonsectarian liberal arts college in Boulder, Colorado, where he and his wife, painter, assemblagist, and book artist Jane Dalrymple-Hollo, make their home.

Hollo's poetry has been widely anthologized, and some of it has been translated into Finnish, French, German, Swedish, and Hungarian.